10·20·30
MINUTES
TO SEW

Nancy Zieman

Published in cooperation with Leisure Arts.

Library of Congress Number: 92-64194
ISBN: 0-8487-1153-X
Manufactured in the United States of America
First Printing 1992

Editor-in-Chief: Nancy J. Fitzpatrick
Senior Crafts Editor: Susan Ramey Wright
Senior Editor, Editorial Services: Olivia Kindig Wells
Director of Manufacturing: Jerry Higdon
Art Director: James Boone

10, 20, 30 Minutes to Sew with Nancy Zieman

Editor: Linda Baltzell Wright
Assistant Editor: Carol Logan Newbill
Editorial Assistant: Roslyn Oneille Hardy
Copy Chief: Mary Jean Haddin
Copy Editor: Susan Smith Cheatham
Production Manager: Rick Litton
Associate Production Manager: Theresa L. Beste
Production Assistant: Pam Beasley Bullock
Designer: Melinda Ponder Goode
Senior Photographer: John O'Hagan
Photostylist: Katie Stoddard

Cover Fabric: "Seltz Paisley" by Schumacher

Dedicated to **Rich,**
the man who smiles and isn't
angered when he's referred to
as "Mr. Nancy."

Special thanks to...

Gail Brown, *sewing journalist and special friend, for her initial edit and countless words of advice, especially in the serging chapter.*

Donna Fenske *and* **Phyllis Steinbach,** *Nancy's Notions Production Department, for their expert sewing skills.*

Betsy Johnson, *Marketing Assistant, for never complaining when making the seemingly end-less changes on my manuscript.*

Rochelle Stibb, *artist and sewing enthusiast, for her attention to sewing detail.*

Contents

*S*ewing: *For me it's a creative outlet and the best therapy I know. I love being able to spend some time in my sewing room to relax and unwind at the end of a busy day.*

Yet like you, I don't have hours to spend sewing every day. Usually there are just a few minutes here or there—10, 20, or 30 minutes, maybe—if I'm really lucky. These precious minutes are a dose of sanity in a far too hectic world. Plus, after several sessions at my machine, I have something to show for my time. It's amazing how just a few minutes a day add up to completed projects!

On my desk I have a calendar with a motivational or thought-provoking verse for each day. I marked the one that says, "Who uses minutes has hours to use; who loses minutes whole years must lose."

I hope that 10-20-30 Minutes To Sew *will inspire you to use your extra minutes to cultivate and enjoy the art of sewing.*

Nancy Zieman

Minutes
TO ORGANIZE

Like you, I struggle to find time to sew. Yet I find that even on busy days, I can free up 10, 20, or 30 minutes. You can do it, too. If you learn to think in these time units, you'll be amazed at how efficient and enjoyable sewing can be!

Several of these 10-, 20-, or 30-minute units can be completed before you ever sit down at your sewing machine or serger. (Machine stitching actually constitutes only a fraction of your total "sewing" time.) Here are some ways to group garment construction steps into units of 30 minutes or less, maximizing your precious sewing time.

Note from Nancy

My favorite interfacings are Stacy's Easy Knit (obviously for knits, but great for light-weight wovens, too), Pellon Sof-Shape (for tailoring), and Fusible Pellon for Feather to Midweight Fabrics (for lightweight woven fabrics). But there are many other fusible interfacings. Check the interfacing section of your favorite fabric store, department store, or catalog.

Timesaving Notions

If your fusibles are already wrinkled, use an Appliqué Pressing Sheet to help press out the wrinkles. Although this non-stick product is generally used when bonding fusible webbing to the wrong side of a fabric or appliqué, it has another use: Place the resin side of the wrinkled fusible interfacing against the Appliqué Pressing Sheet. Press. The interfacing will temporarily stick to the sheet. After waiting a few seconds for the fusible to cool, peel the fusible from the sheet. Presto! No more wrinkles.

Supplies:
STOCK UP NOW TO SAVE TIME LATER

Keep a stock of basic supplies such as interfacing, thread, zippers, and buttons on hand, eliminating time-consuming return trips to the store.

Fusible Interfacings

Use fusible interfacings to save time and effort. "Fusibles," as they are commonly called, are treated with a special heat-activated resin. When pressed, the resin-treated side of the fusible will be permanently bonded to the fashion fabric with no stitching at all. Purchase 3 to 4 yards of interfacing at a time. Keep a variety of interfacings in your inventory, so that you'll have appropriate types available for a range of fabric weights—sheer, light, medium, and heavy. When you get your fusible interfacing home, roll it on a cardboard tube so that it won't get wrinkled during storage. Since interfacings vary in the amount of time, heat, and moisture needed for fusing, save the interleaf instructions (the how-tos printed on thin vinyl rolled with the interfacing on the bolt). You can slip the interleaf inside the storage tube for a handy reference.

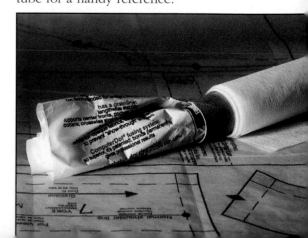

Threads

Whenever possible, buy large economy spools in colors that match or blend with your favorite fabric colors. An example: If your wardrobe includes several shades of red, keep red thread on hand. (Remember, for the best match, choose thread a shade or 2 darker than your fabric.)

When winding bobbins in basic colors, wind several at a time. You'll use 1 or 2 bobbins per project and still have a spare. That's a lot faster than running out of bobbin thread, unthreading your machine, winding the bobbin, and rethreading!

Zippers

Consider buying zippers "by the yard" or stocking up on commonly used colors. Buy a zipper longer than required—it can always be shortened to the exact length desired.

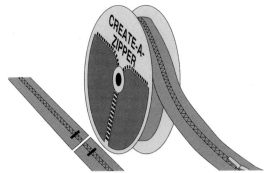

Other Basic Notions

The most productive seamstresses I know always have other basic notions—elastics, buttons, linings, snaps, hooks and eyes—on hand, too. Again, stick with your basic or favorite accent colors (or shades that blend with them), and you'll be surprised at how well these on-hand notions coordinate with different projects.

Organize
TASKS INTO TIME UNITS

Note from Nancy

To identify the fabrics that have been pretreated, clip a small corner off the pretreated fabric—a signal that it's ready for sewing.

Pretreat Your Fabric
—20 *Minutes*—

I recommend pretreating fabrics right after purchasing them, so that they will be "ready for the needle." Though this may seem unnecessary, the better-safe-than-sorry rule is "Pretreat the fabric as you will wash or clean the finished garment." Here's why:

• Even shrink-resistant fabrics may shrink when machine-washed and dried. Even "Dry-clean-only" fabrics should be professionally steamed, or at the least, thoroughly steam-pressed at home. By removing any residual shrinkage before cutting out the garment, you will ensure consistent fit throughout the life of the garment.

• Most fabric mills add finishes to fabrics to prevent soiling and wrinkling. Unfortunately, these resin finishes can also cause the machine to skip stitches. Pretreating fabrics helps remove these resins and prevent the aggravation of skipped stitches.

• Pretreating will also tell you whether washing or steam pressing will remove the center crease and wrinkles. If the creases don't disappear, avoid those areas when laying out the pattern pieces.

Guidelines for Pretreating Washable Fabric

When you purchase fabric, be sure to read the care-code label on the end of the fabric bolt. The following list gives the code numbers and explains what they mean.

1	Machine wash warm
2	Machine wash warm, line dry
3	Machine wash warm, tumble dry, remove promptly
4	Machine wash warm, delicate cycle, tumble dry low, use cool iron
5	Machine wash warm, do not dry clean
6	Hand wash separately, use cool iron
7	Dry clean only
8	Dry clean pile fabric method only
9	Wipe with damp cloth only
10	Machine wash warm, tumble dry or line dry

• Launder washable fabrics in the delicate cycle of your washing machine. It isn't necessary to wash a full cycle; a short cycle with a small amount of detergent works just as well.

• If the fabric ravels considerably, zigzag or serge the raw edges before washing.

• Dry the fabric as it will be dried after the garment is completed.

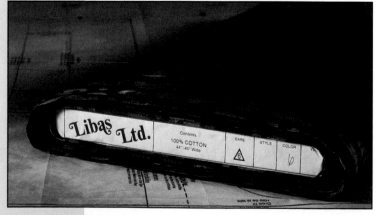

Read the care-code label.

Store All Your Project "Ingredients" Together

10 Minutes

Once you have stocked up on interfacings, threads, zippers, and other notions, gather those needed for your project and store them with the pattern and fabric. (Check the back of the pattern envelope for other recommended notions, to make sure you haven't missed anything.) Now the materials will all be ready and waiting when you have another 10, 20, or 30 minutes to sew. Try 1 of these tried-and-true storage methods:

• Wrap the smaller project ingredients inside the fabric and place the fabric on a shelf or in a drawer near your sewing area. Put the easiest-to-misplace items, such as buttons or hooks and eyes, in a regular mailing envelope.

Or

• Enclose all items in a large bag. Clear plastic works best, so that you can see the contents.

Or

• Store fabric, notions, and the pattern in an inexpensive plastic storage basket or bin (sold at most discount and variety stores). This is my favorite method and also the storage method we use in the dressmaking department at Nancy's Notions, Ltd.

After you've collected everything required for your sewing project, you're ready for the next step.

Note from Nancy

Use waxed paper and permanent felt-tip pens for altering patterns. They are inexpensive and readily available. Another plus: After the alterations are completed, the waxed paper can easily be fused to the original pattern.

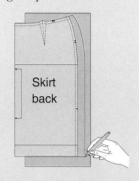

Skirt back

Timesaving Notions

Pattern weights come in all shapes and sizes. Some are round washer-like weights; some are shaped to fit pattern angles and curves, while still others are molded in the shape of sewing paraphernalia. Regardless of shape and size, all pattern weights save time by reducing the number of pins required to secure the pattern pieces.

Prepare All Pattern Pieces
—10 Minutes—

Another sewing unit that takes 10 minutes or less is cutting apart the pattern pieces for the project you have chosen. At this point, cutting accuracy is not crucial. Here's all you need to do:

- Cut out the pieces needed for your project.
- Refold any unused pieces. Replace them in the pattern envelope.
- Press the pieces you'll be using with a warm, dry iron. (Steam may cause the pattern tissue to ripple.)
- Drape the pieces you'll be using over a hanger, pinning smaller pattern pieces to larger ones. Place the pattern envelope in a plastic bag, hole-punched at the top; hang the bag over the hanger hook.

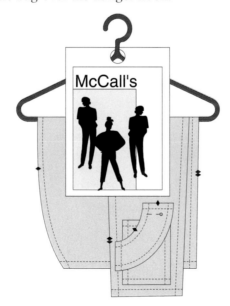

Alter the Pattern
—20 Minutes—

Few of us are a perfect size 10. To make a pattern fit, most of us need to add to 1 body area or subtract from another. When you can find a 20-minute time block, alter your pattern, readying it for layout and cutting.

Use your favorite method of altering the pattern to your measurements and height. If you generally use patterns from the same

company (such as Butterick or McCall's), you may be able to repeat the same basic alterations from garment to garment.

A recipe card file is an efficient way to keep track of your alterations. On each card, list the pattern number and any adjustments made. Date the card so that you can see at a glance when the pattern was last used. Have you gained or lost weight since

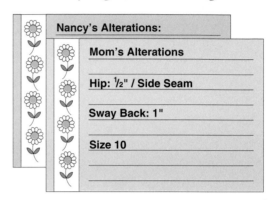

that time? Then you'll be alerted to readjust your alterations before using the pattern again.

You'll save time by adding recipe cards for other people, too. If you sew for your children, mother, husband, or other relatives or friends, these cards will serve as quick references for necessary alterations.

Cut Out the Garment
—30 Minutes—

When you have a 30-minute time slot available, reserve that time for cutting out your sewing project. Streamline the cutting-out session by following these timesaving strategies:

Two Layers at the Same Time

If you're making a lined skirt, stack the skirt and lining fabrics and cut out both at once. Or cut out 2 blouses at the same time. Here are some guidelines for "stacking" fabrics:

- The fabrics must be the same width.
- The fabrics should be no heavier than medium-weight. Heavier fabrics, when stacked, are too bulky to cut easily and accurately.
- Pin the 2 fabric layers together along the folded and selvage edges before laying

out the pattern.
• Place slippery fabrics on top.
Note: Fabrics that require matching, such as plaids and stripes, cannot be stacked.

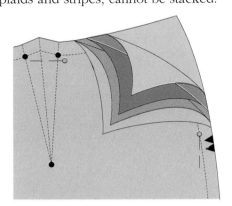

Pattern Weights

• Begin by pinning 1 end of the grain line arrow on each pattern piece. Measure from the arrow to the selvage or fold. Shift the pattern, if necessary, until the other end of the arrow measures the same distance from the selvage or fold. (See diagram on opposite page.) Pin the pattern piece in place.
• Use weights to secure the remaining pattern edges. Position the weights near the edges of 1 piece and cut it out. Then move the weights to another piece; cut. Repeat until all pieces are cut.

Adjoining Cutting Lines

Whenever possible, place straight cutting lines adjacent to each other—you'll be able to make 1 cut for both lines. For example, you can cut the lower edge of a top and the upper edge of a cuff simultaneously. (Check to be certain grain lines correspond.)

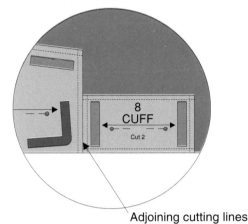

Adjoining cutting lines

Sharp Shears and Scissors

For best results, use 8" dressmaker shears for cutting fabrics. Sharpen the shears periodically to ensure clean-cut edges. Use a sharpening stone to hone cutting edges and prevent dull spots. Reserve these shears for cutting only fabric.

Note from Nancy

I am frequently asked to explain the difference between scissors and shears. Shears, perfect for cutting out fabric, have blades more than 6" long and differently shaped handle bows or loops, 1 to fit the thumb and a larger loop to fit 2 or more fingers. Scissors, perfect for trimming, snipping, and crafts, have blades less than 6" long and identical bows (for finger and thumb).

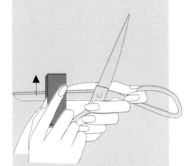

Timesaving Notions

Use Gingher's sharpening stone to maintain your precious sewing shears and scissors. Work along the beveled surface of the knife edge blade, sliding the stone upward, working from the tip of the blade to the shank. After honing, wipe the blade clean.

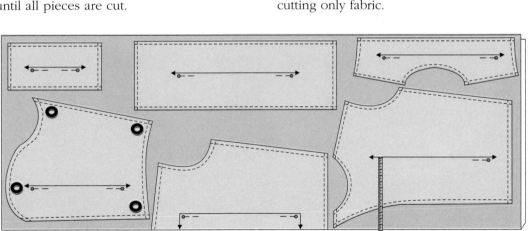

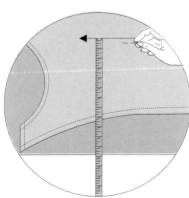

Pin the pattern to the fabric at the grain line arrows. Use pattern weights to secure the remaining pattern edges.

15

Rotary Cutting Tools

Rotary cutters, cutting boards, and gridded rulers have changed the way home sewers, fabric crafters, and quilters cut fabric. In seconds, rotary cutters—in combination with a cutting board and ruler—can accurately slice through several layers of fabric.

Rotary cutters are available in 2 sizes. The heavy-duty model used by most quilters has a blade diameter of 2¾" (or 45 mm). The smaller size has a blade diameter of 1⅛" (or 28 mm). To cut out pattern pieces, use the smaller cutter (which provides greater maneuverability around curved areas) for light-to midweight fabrics. Save the larger cutter for straight pieces and/or heavier fabrics. You'll be amazed at how much time you save when cutting out smaller pattern pieces, interfacings, ribbings, and children's garments.

When you are cutting with a rotary cutter, using a gridded cutting board or mat is a must. The mat, made of a special "self-healing" material that is not damaged by the cutting blade, protects the surface of your work table. Look for rectangular sizes from 6" x 18" up to 36" x 48". Larger boards are easier to work with—it's a good idea to buy the largest size you can afford.

The third essential tool is a ruler. Transparent, gridded Plexiglas rulers, made especially for use with rotary cutters, are available in a wide variety of sizes, ranging from a 4" x 4" square to a 6" x 24" rectangle.

Marking the Garment Pieces

—— *10 Minutes* ——

It's easy to fit this 10-minute unit in before going to work in the morning, while waiting for dinner to finish cooking, or while your children are taking a nap.

Since your garment will probably be constructed in several separate blocks of time, markings serve as indispensable reminders of construction details and matching points.

Nip Markings

Nip notches instead of cutting them outward. Make short ¼" clips into seam allowances. (Be careful not to clip deeper than ¼", in case alterations are required after the first fitting.)

- Nip-mark the ends of darts within the seam allowance. Mark the points of darts with chalk or a washable marking pen. Do not clip the dart points!

V-Clip Markings

- Use V-clips to indicate center backs and fronts on the garment, collars, and facings.
- Make V-clips ¼" to ⅜" deep. If the center front or center back is on the fold, simply angle-cut along the fold; when the piece is opened flat, you'll see that a V shape has been formed.
- Make a ¼" V-clip in each side seam allowance to indicate the garment hemline.

Pen/Pencil/Chalk Markings

- Use water- or air-soluble marking pens/pencils, chalk, or chalk wheels for marking darts, pleats, buttonhole/button placements, and circle or dot pattern markings.
- Mark on the wrong side of the fabric.
- Indicate the right side of the fabric if it's difficult to distinguish the right side from the wrong side. Mark within the seam allowance with chalk or a water-soluble marking pen.
- After sewing, remove the water-soluble markings with a dab of water. Air-soluble pens have purple markings that vanish without washing in 12 to 24 hours.

Note from Nancy

Corresponding notches on the pattern have the same number. To further identify which notches go together, mark the notch numbers within the seam allowance with a washable marking pen or tailor's chalk. When sewing the seams, it will be easy for you to determine which pieces go together.

Note from Nancy

I use marking pens almost every time I sew. But a word of caution: Quilters have discovered that the ink marks may reappear many years later, so avoid using these pens on heirloom-quality projects. Also, the heat of an iron will set the marks; remove the marks before pressing.

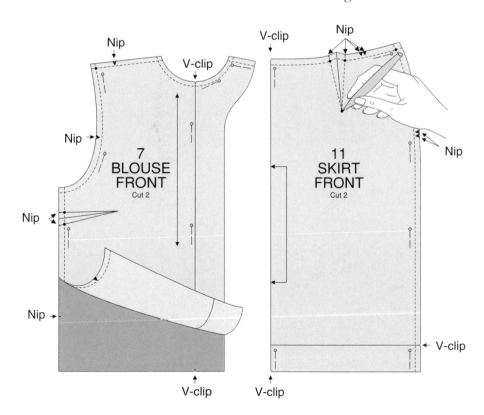

Note from Nancy

Rayon velvet is one of the few fabrics on which fusible interfacings cannot be used; the fiber and pile weave cannot withstand the fusing temperature or iron pressure. The same may hold true for some delicate silks. Test to ensure fusing success (see "Fusible Interfacing Test Swatch" at right).

Interfacing Guide

GARMENTS	FABRICS	FUSIBLE INTERFACING
Separates and Dresses (sheer shaping)	voile, chiffon, lawn, gauze, batiste, leno, georgette dimity, crepe de chine, charmeuse	Pellon Fusible #906 Sheer D'Light Featherweight
(soft shaping)	challis, jersey, single knits, tricot, crepe	Pellon Fusible #911FF Pellon Easy Shaper #114ES Sheer D'Light Lightweight
(crisp shaping)	shirtings, gingham, poplin, chambray, seersucker, cotton, broadcloth, cord, oxford cloth, piqué, lightweight linen, cotton blends, ciré, lightweight denim	Pellon Fusible #931TD Pellon ShirTailor #950F Stacy Shape-flex #101SF Form-flex All-purpose Sheer D'Light Mediumweight Armo Shirt-Shaper Shape Maker All-Purpose Shirt Maker
Coats, Dresses, Jackets, and Suits (all-over shaping)	wool, linen, denim, poplin, corduroy, tweeds, flannels, wool blends, gabardine, mohair, synthetic leather, suede	Pellon Sof-Shape #880F Armo Fusi-Form Lightweight Shape-up Lightweight Suit Maker
(crisp shaping)		Pellon Pel-Aire #881F Armo Fusi-Form Suitweight Armo Form-Flex Nonwoven Shape-Up Suitweight
Knits Only	double knits, cotton, or blended knits, single knits, lightweight sweater knits, terry, jersey, lightweight velour, sweatshirt fleece	Pellon Stretch-Ease #921F Stacy Easy Knit 130EK Fusi-Knit Knit Fuze

Test and Apply Fusible Interfacing

Fusible interfacings are suitable for most fabrics. In 1 fast pressing step, they add the shape and stability essential to the look, fit, and long-term durability of your garment. You'll enjoy working with them!

Choose an interfacing weight that's compatible with your fashion fabric. Fusibles are available in weights ranging from very light, for use with delicate lightweight fabrics, to heavy, for use with woolens and wool blends. Check the label on the end of the bolt and the interfacing guide below for use suggestions.

As a general rule, choose fusible interfacing 1 weight lighter than your fashion fabric. For example, if using a medium-weight fabric, choose a lightweight fusible interfacing. (Keep in mind that the fusing resins add weight that is unnoticeable until the interfacing is fused to the fabric.)

Fusible Interfacing Test Swatch

To determine whether a fusible is suitable for your fabric and how long it will take to fuse, make a test swatch. This is especially important if you are using a new interfacing or fabric or are combining an interfacing and fabric for the first time.

1. Cut a 4" square of both the fusible interfacing and fabric.

2. Place the wrong side of the fabric next to the resin-treated side of the interfacing.

3. Place a 1" square of fabric at 1 corner, between the fashion fabric and interfacing. You will use this fabric square as a "handle" to test the fusion of interfacing and fashion fabric.

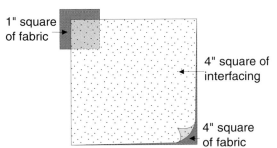

1" square of fabric

4" square of interfacing

4" square of fabric

4. With the non-resin side of the interfacing swatch up, fuse the interfacing for 10 to 15 seconds, using a steam iron set at the wool temperature.

5. After the test square cools, try to peel the interfacing from the fashion fabric, using the fabric "handle" you fused in place. If you can easily separate the layers, it's an indication that the interfacing did not fuse properly. Increase fusing time, pressure, and/or temperature.

6. Check the appearance of both right and wrong sides of the interfaced test square. Look for bubbles, wrinkles, or discoloration on the right side of the fabric square. Also check the feel of the interfaced fabric—has the interfacing added too much weight? If so, test a lighter weight interfacing.

Make Your Own Interfacing Pattern Pieces

Some patterns don't include separate interfacing pattern pieces for units such as collars and shirt cuffs. But using separate interfacing patterns saves interfacing and saves cutting time because you don't have to trim away the seam allowances. Make your own interfacing patterns using waxed paper and a 6" hem gauge.

1. Place the pattern piece on a padded surface, such as a tablecloth or an extra length of fabric.

2. Cover the pattern with a piece of waxed paper.

3. Use the hem gauge to "draw" along the cutting line. Set the hem gauge at ½". Guide the end point of the gauge along the pattern cutting line. The gauge will automatically make 2 lines on the waxed paper: an outer line along the original pattern cutting line and an inner line at the ½" marking. Use the inner line as your interfacing cutting line. The fusible interfacing pattern should be ½" smaller than the fabric pattern piece so that the interfacing will be caught in the ⅝" seam allowance when the seams are stitched.

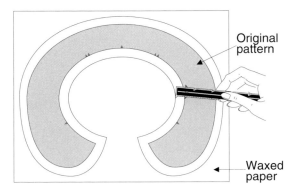

Original pattern

Waxed paper

4. In areas such as the outer edge of a facing, the interfacing should extend to the outer edge of the original pattern piece. When making the interfacing pattern, with the hem gauge, trace only along the pattern's outer edge.

Interfacing pattern line

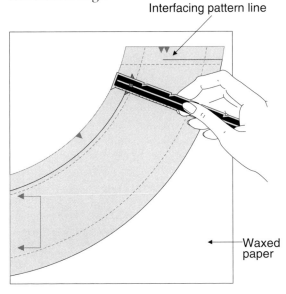

Waxed paper

5. Label the waxed paper interfacing pattern with the name of the pattern piece, the pattern number, and the size. Store it with the pattern.

Fuse Interfacing to the Fabric

1. Center the interfacing on the fashion fabric piece, placing the resin side of the fusible interfacing on the wrong side of the fabric.

2. Steam-baste the interfacing in place before permanently fusing. Use the tip of your iron to position the interfacing and secure it to the fabric in a few key areas.

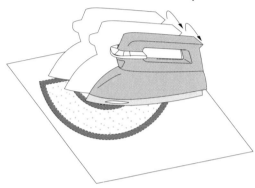

3. Fuse the interfacing following the manufacturer's instructions. Press with an up-and-down motion. General guidelines for fusing are as follows:

• Set the iron at wool temperature.

• Protect the fabric and interfacing with a press cloth. A transparent press cloth allows you to see the fabric while fusing; watch to see that the interfacing hasn't shifted or creased.

• Use steam or dampen the press cloth. Press with the non-resin side of the interfacing up.

• Fuse for 10-15 seconds.

• Apply sufficient pressure. This is the most important step and is commonly overlooked. If the fabric has a bubbly appearance after fusing, insufficient pressure is probably the cause. Try fusing again, putting more pressure on the iron.

Divide Pattern Pieces Into Construction Units
10 Minutes

When you have another 10 minutes to spare, divide your garment pieces into construction units. When sewing, I don't necessarily follow the sewing sequence given on the pattern guide sheet. I read through the pattern guide sheet and jot down the sewing units as I see them. Units like a collar, cuffs, and sleeves could easily be sewn before sewing the main garment pieces together. When I have time to sew, I choose a sewing unit that corresponds with the time I have to spend and a project that fits my sewing mood! (Remember, think of sewing time in terms of minutes, not hours.)

• Divide the garment pieces into a separate stack for each unit.

• Make a list of the units and the general sewing steps in that unit.

• Check off the units as you complete them; then you can immediately see your progress.

Possible units for a blouse might include:
• Collar:
    Stitch the outer seams.
    Edgestitch (optional).
• Cuffs:
    Stitch the outer seams.
    Edgestitch (optional).
• Sleeves:
    Stitch or serge the underarm seam.
    Ease the fullness of the sleeve cap.
    Attach the cuff to the lower edge of the sleeve.
• Pleats and seams:
    Stitch and press the front pleats.
    Stitch or serge the yoke to the front and back blouse pieces.
    Stitch or serge the side seams.
• Set in the sleeves:
    Pin the sleeves to the armhole.
    Stitch the sleeve in place.
    Press.
    Trim and restitch the underarm area.
• Buttonholes:
    Mark buttonhole positions on the blouse front.
    Make a test sample. Stitch the buttonholes.
• Hem:
    Fold up the hem and topstitch.
• Handwork:
    Stitch buttons at the front placket and cuffs.

Possible units for a skirt might include:
• Pockets
• Seams:
    Stitch or serge all side seams.
    Zigzag or turn under the seam edges.
    Press open the seam allowances.

• Elastic waistband:
  Stitch the casing.
  Insert the elastic.
• Hem:
  Press up the hem allowance.
  Machine-stitch hem with a double
  needle, or handstitch.

Set Up Your Machine
10 Minutes

When it's finally time to sew, take 10 minutes to clean and set up your sewing machine (and serger, if you use one). Cleaning and oiling your machine before each project reduces the likelihood of mechanical problems during garment construction.

Prepare Your Sewing Machine

• Change the machine needle. (In my opinion, this is the most important part of getting the machine ready.) Sometimes you may think the old needle is in good condition. However, there may be tiny burrs and imperfections that are unnoticeable to the naked eye. A new needle costs only pennies and prevents uneven stitching and disastrous fabric snags.
• Remove the bobbin.
• Brush out the bobbin area. (This prevents lint from clogging the machine.)

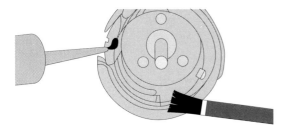

• Apply a drop of oil to the bobbin area. (Consult your owner's manual for specifics.)
• Wind the bobbin(s) and thread the machine.

Prepare Your Serger

• Brush out the area around the feed dogs. (This is especially important on a serger, because the machine both stitches and trims fabric. Lint quickly accumulates and can jam the machine and/or reduce stitch quality.)

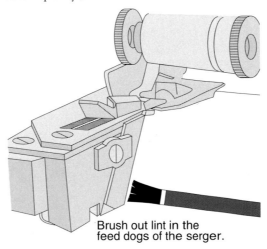

Brush out lint in the feed dogs of the serger.

• Change threads. See Chapter 3, "Serging, the Ultimate Time-Saver."
• Check the needles. Some sergers use sewing machine needles, while others use stronger needles designed for industrial sergers. If your serger uses regular sewing machine needles, change the needles with each project just as you do on your sewing machine. If the serger uses industrial needles, plan to change needles every 2 to 3 projects. Of course, if a needle is worn, damaged, or causes skipped stitches, replace it now!

Fast
FASHION
ELEMENTS

Now it's time to sew! Here are some ways to make the most of your sewing time by refining the pattern guide sheet instructions. Don't worry—streamlining the process doesn't mean compromising the results. In fact, I think that after trying some of these how-tos, you'll agree that these faster techniques improve the look and fit of your garments.

Collar CONNECTIONS

Note from Nancy

When I am using medium-weight or heavier fabric, I like to use a multi-zigzag stitch for the understitching. There are more stitches per inch, creating a crisper collar edge.

Wrapped Corner Collars

—*20 Minutes*—

To eliminate bulk from a collar, sew the outer edges in 3 steps. I call this the "wrapped-corner technique," and it definitely ranks as one of my favorites. You, too, will be pleased with the great-looking results—in minutes.

Patterns for tailored shirts, blouses, and jackets generally include pieces for both upper and under collars. Casual-wear patterns, however, usually provide only 1 pattern piece for the collar. (The following instructions assume that your pattern has

separate pieces for upper and lower collars.) Either way, you can use the wrapped-corner technique.

Most guide sheet instructions call for interfacing only 1 collar layer: the under collar when separate pieces are given, and the under half of the collar when a single piece is given. But interfacing both the upper and under collar adds body and strengthens the collar seam. Use a lightweight interfacing, such as Pellon's Feather to Midweight fusible interfacing.

1. Cut out fusible interfacing for both collar pieces, as discussed in Chapter 1. Fuse the interfacing to the wrong side of the collar pieces.

2. With right sides together, pin the upper and under collars along the unnotched edge. Stitch the seam from end to end.

3. Press the seam to 1 side and then press it open.

4. Grade the under collar seam allowance to ¼" and the upper collar seam allowance to ⅜".

5. Press the seam allowances toward the under collar and understitch the entire seam.

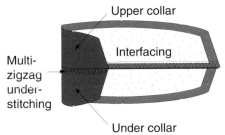

Upper collar

Interfacing

Multi-zigzag under-stitching

Under collar

6. Fold the collar along the seam, with right sides together. The seam allowances will roll toward the under collar. Stitch from the fold to the neckline edge.

7. To minimize bulk, grade the seam allowances and trim the corner allowances at an angle. Press the seams to 1 side and then press them open. Press the corners over a point presser.

8. Turn the collar right side out and machine-baste the open edges together. Press.

Classic Peter Pan Collar

20 Minutes

A Peter Pan collar is a fashion classic, a focal point frequently found on blouses and dresses, especially those designed for children. But there's nothing more distracting than having the under collar roll to the upper side, as they sometimes do. Here are some tips on preventing the problem.

1. To prepare the collar:
   - Cut 4 collar pieces (2 upper collar and 2 under collar pieces), and interface all the pieces.
   - On the under collar pieces only, trim ⅛" from all *outer*, unnotched edges. Do not trim the neck edge. (Trimming is essential to keep the under collar from rolling to the upper side.)
   - With right sides together and outer edges aligned, pin 1 upper collar piece to 1 under collar piece to make 1 half-collar. Repeat for the remaining collar pieces.

2. To stitch the collar pieces together:
   - Stitch with the under collar next to the presser foot and the upper collar next to the feed dogs. This automatically eases the upper collar to fit the smaller under collar. Press the seam to 1 side.
   - Grade the seam, trimming the under collar seam allowances to ¼" and the upper collar seam allowances to ⅜". Turn the collar right side out and press.

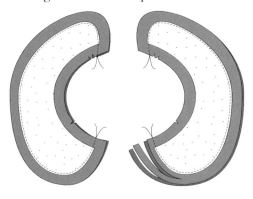

   - From the right side, understitch the seam, sewing all the seam allowances to the under collar. Press.

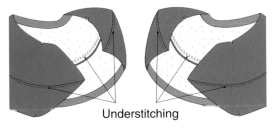

Understitching

3. Apply the collar to the garment, following the guide sheet instructions.

Note from Nancy

When you are sewing together 2 fabric pieces of different lengths, stitch with the longer layer down (next to the feed dogs of the sewing machine) and the shorter layer up (next to the presser foot). The feed dogs will gently and evenly ease the longer layer to meet the shorter layer.

Timesaving Notions

For a pressing template, use a lightweight piece of cardboard cut to the shape of the pattern piece (without seam allowances). The Pocket Curve Template, although generally used to form and press the round curves of a patch pocket, can also do double-duty as a template for the Peter Pan collar.

Pockets
NEW AND IMPROVED

Timesaving Notions

Stay-Tape is a ⅝"-wide, 100%-nylon stabilizing strip. Unlike cotton tapes, it does not have to be preshrunk. It also adds very little bulk and does not ravel.

Timesaving Notions

Try using a Stitch-Along to topstitch pockets. Place the plastic Stitch-Along template along the topstitching line. The plastic teeth on the underside stabilize the template. Guide the presser foot along the Stitch-Along as you sew.

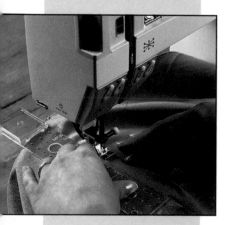

Speedy Sport Pockets

—— *20 Minutes* ——

You've undoubtedly seen this pocket on sport shorts and pants. The technique is fast, and the look is figure flattering. (There's only 1 pocket-lining layer, so bulk is minimized.) To add pockets to your favorite pattern, make a few simple modifications in the pattern.

1. Use nip markings or a washable marker to indicate the pocket openings on the side seams of the pant front pattern.

2. Make a pocket-lining pattern—a rectangle about 7" by 10". Cut 1 pocket-lining piece from the fashion fabric for each pocket.

3. To prepare the pant front:
• Mark the pocket notches and dots on the fabric pant front.
• Fold the seam allowance to the wrong side and press.
• Trim the seam allowance to ¼" between the pocket opening markings.
• Cut a piece of Stay-Tape or twill tape slightly longer than the pocket opening. Pin the tape over the gap where the seam allowance was trimmed. (Stay-Tape clean-finishes the pocket and supports the edge.)
• From the right side, topstitch the Stay-Tape on all sides, catching the pocket sides in the stitching.

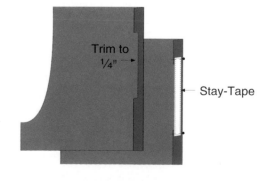

7"

Pocket Lining

10"

Trim to ¼"

Stay-Tape

4. With right sides together and nip markings aligned, place the pocket lining on the pant back. Stitch, using ⅝" seams. Press the seam allowances toward the pocket. Then press the pocket lining toward the pant back.

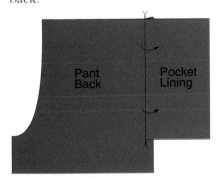

5. To stitch the pant front to the pant back:

• With right sides up, lay the pant back and pocket lining flat. At the seam line, place the pant front on the pocket lining as shown.

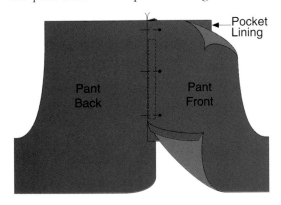

• To sew the pant front to the back, topstitch above and below the pocket-opening, aligning and connecting with the pocket topstitching.

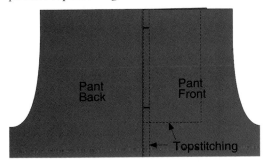

• Where the topstitching lines meet, use a narrow, short zigzag and stitch across at the top and bottom of pocket opening.

6. To form the pocket, from the right side, topstitch the pocket lining to the pant front as shown.

Professional Patch Pocket

—— 20 Minutes ——

Here's a way to complete a patch pocket, with beautifully mitered corners, in only 20 minutes. Believe it or not, the secret to success is transparent tape—the same easy-to-remove tape you keep tucked in your kitchen catchall drawer. Transparent tape is a terrific way to sew accurate mitered corners. The tape serves 2 purposes: It holds the fabric edges together and provides an easy-to-follow guide for straight stitching.

1. To miter the bottom pocket corners:

• Measure and mark 1¼" (twice the seam width) from each side of both lower pocket corners.

Timesaving Notions
To quickly press open seam allowances at corners, use a point presser. Place the seam over the pointed end of the point presser and press.

• Place transparent tape between the 2 marks on the wrong side of the fabric, extending the tape ends as shown.

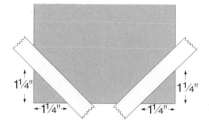

• With right sides together, fold the corner to a point, aligning the marks and the tape. Stitch next to the tape but not through it, forming the miter.

• Trim the seam ¼" to ⅜" from the stitching. Repeat for the other corner.

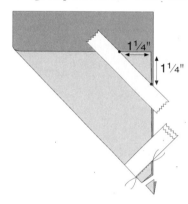

2. Turn the pocket right side out. Press the seam allowances to the wrong side.

3. Fuse interfacing to the hem allowance.

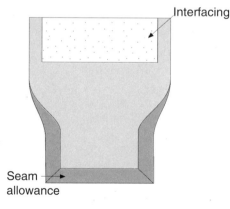

Interfacing

Seam allowance

4. Stitch the side seams of the pocket hem. Press the seams to 1 side and then press them open. Grade the seams and trim the corners at an angle. Turn the pocket right side out and press.

5. To apply the pocket to the garment:

• Cut ¼" strips of Wonder-Under for web basting. This eliminates the need to stitch over pins, which may cause uneven topstitching lines. A rotary cutter and mat make cutting the web easy, or you can use the ½" pre-cut strips of Wonder-Under and cut them down the middle.

• On the inside of the pocket, position the web strips on the seam allowances, about ¼" to ⅜" inside the pocket-edge fold. (The web side of Wonder-Under should be next to the fabric, with the paper side up.) Press the strips in place and then peel off the paper backing.

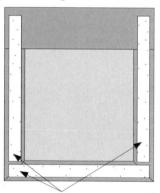

Strips of Wonder-Under

• Position the pocket on the garment. Cover with a press cloth and press to fuse-baste the pocket to the garment.

6. To edgestitch the pocket:

• Replace your machine's standard presser foot with a blindhem foot.

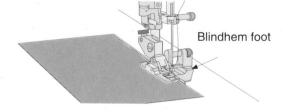

Blindhem foot

• On the right side of the pocket, edgestitch close to the side and bottom edges of the pocket, using the fabric fold as a guide for the blindhem foot.

All-in-One Slenderizing Side Pocket

10 Minutes

In only 10 minutes, you can add side pockets to any skirt, pants, or shorts. Traditionally, separate pocket pieces are stitched to the garment front and back sections. To save time and reduce bulk, make my all-in-one side pocket: Cut out the pocket as part of the garment. These pockets add no weight to the hip area because there are no pocket seams to create extra bulk. So the pockets are perfectly flattering and perfect for light- to medium-weight fabrics.

1. To modify the pattern and eliminate the pocket seam:

• Make a duplicate of the pocket pattern piece out of tissue or waxed paper, transferring the stitching lines, notches, and dot markings. (Now you have a pocket pattern to join to the front garment piece and a duplicate for the back garment piece.)

• Place the original pocket pattern piece on the garment front pattern piece, aligning the stitching lines. Match any notches and/or dot markings. Pin or tape the pocket pattern and garment pattern together. Repeat for the duplicate pocket pattern piece and the garment back piece.

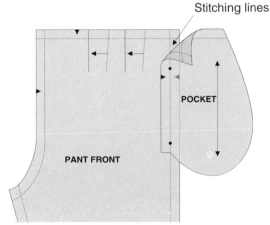

2. Position the modified pattern pieces on the fabric. Cut them out.

3. To stitch the garment pieces together:

• Align the garment/pocket fronts and backs and stitch from the bottom hem edge to the dot marking the lower pocket opening. Pivot and continue stitching around the pocket to the waistline edge.

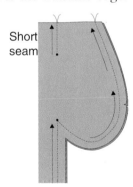

• Stitch the short seam from the upper pocket opening to the waistline. No more bulky pocket seams!

Note from Nancy

Because you tape the pocket pattern to the garment pattern and cut it out as 1 piece, you may need additional fabric for the wider pieces. Give the layout sketches on the guide sheet a quick scan before cutting out the pattern. Try repositioning the pattern pieces or refolding the fabric to utilize every square inch. If you haven't purchased your fabric yet, buy 1/4 yard extra of 60"-wide fabric and 1/2 yard extra of 45"-wide fabric.

Flatter Pocket Flaps
20 Minutes

Most pocket flaps are lined, so that there is a seam at each side. The following technique alters the seam position, making the flap faster to sew, flatter, and less bulky.

1. Use the original flap pattern to cut fusible interfacing for each pocket flap as detailed in Chapter 1.

2. Now create a new flap pattern:

• Photocopy or trace a second flap pattern.

• Machine-baste the 2 paper pattern flaps together along each side seam line.

• On the top flap, mark a new vertical seam. (This will eliminate the bulk of seams at the sides. If the center of the flap tapers to a V, avoid placing the new seam there.)

• Cut along the marked line and open the pattern.

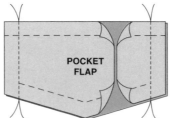

• Tape a ⅝"-wide seam allowance to each side of the new flap pattern.

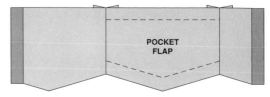

3. Use this new pattern to cut the pocket flaps from your fabric. (This 1 flap piece is all you need.) Cut out a fabric flap for each pocket.

4. Fuse the interfacing to the wrong side of the original pocket flap.

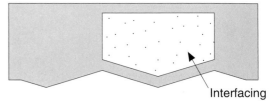

Interfacing

5. To stitch the pocket flap:

• With right sides together, stitch the vertical seam. Trim and grade the seam allowances and then press them open.

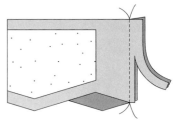

• Refold the pocket flap, aligning the lower edges. Stitch the lower edge seam.

• Grade the seam and turn the flap right side out. At the side edges, the flap will be folded rather than seamed. (You'll love the flat and smooth way the flap lies on the garment—and on you.) You may edgestitch the flap if you wish.

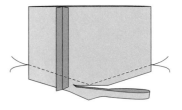

6. Apply the pocket flap to the garment following the guide sheet instructions.

Streamlined
SLEEVES

Easiest Sleeve Easing
10 Minutes

Here's a little-known yet tried-and-true technique you can use to ease set-in sleeves quickly. Use 2 pencils with erasers to ease the fullness from the sleeve cap! You'll find that this "eraser easing" is faster and more accurate than the traditional basted easing. And once the sleeve cap is eased, it's fast and easy to set the sleeve into the arm-hole—free of puckers.

1. Place the sleeve under the presser foot at 1 of the notch positions. Lower the needle into the fabric, about ½" from the fabric's edge.

2. Place 1 pencil eraser on the fabric on each side of the presser foot, just in front of the needle.

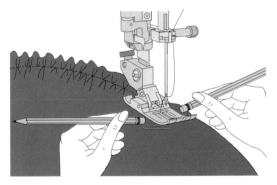

3. Pull the erasers outward, away from the presser foot, as you stitch around the sleeve cap, forcing the fabric to stretch on the bias. Stitch a small section and reposition the erasers. Continue stitching to the next notch. (If you prefer, you may use your fingers to pull the fabric instead of using erasers, but erasers have more grip.)

Fold-and-Stitch Hem

10 Minutes

Short sleeves can be hemmed in minutes, using this quick fold-and-stitch technique. The hem edge is hidden inside the tuck, durable and ravel-free for the life of the garment. For easier maneuvering, hem the sleeve before setting it into the armhole.

1. Stitch the underarm seam of the sleeve. Press the seam to 1 side and then press it open.

2. Clip the seam allowances at the hemline and then trim the seam allowances to ¼", from the hemline to the lower edge of the sleeve.

3. Fold up the hem allowance and press.

4. Then fold up this hem allowance again. Press.

5. Stitch ¼" from the second fold, catching the raw edge of the hem and creating a tuck.

6. Turn the hem down and the tuck up; press.

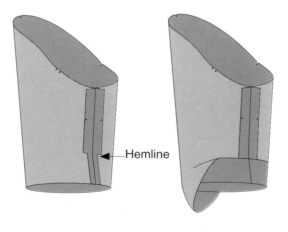

Hemline

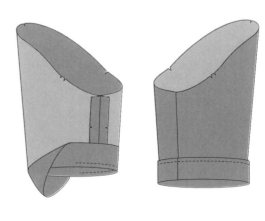

Faster ZIPPERS, WAISTBANDS & FACINGS

Quick Two-Seam Lapped Zipper

—— 20 Minutes ——

If your previous experiences with inserting zippers were enough to make your blood boil, relax! Eliminate the hassle with this updated technique. It requires only an increased seam allowance, 2 rows of machine stitching, and a little pressing.

1. Purchase the zipper at least 1" to 2" longer than needed. For example, if the pattern calls for a 7" zipper, purchase a 9" zipper. This additional length allows you to extend the zipper beyond the top of the garment during construction, assuring even stitching in the zipper tab area.

2. To increase the zipper seam allowance:

• Add ⅜" to the seam allowance in the zipper area (for a total of 1") as you are cutting out the pattern. This wider seam allowance gives you more fabric to work with, so that you don't run out when stitching the lap of the zipper.

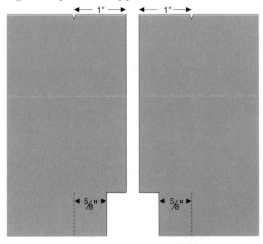

Timesaving Notions

Pins sometimes create dimples in the fabric, so that the completed stitching is not perfectly straight. I like to use strips of Sewer's Fix-It Tape about 4" apart to position the lap. This ½"-wide tape keeps the edge perfectly flat and results in a more even topstitching. When you're finished, the tape can be easily removed, leaving no sticky residue.

• Cut a ¼" V-clip to mark the stitching line at the top of the zipper opening on both the left and right seam allowances. These markings are extremely important.

3. Stitch the lower portion of the seam into which the zipper will be inserted, stopping at the dot marking the zipper opening and its wider seam allowance. Lock your stitching at the dot by sewing in place several times with the machine's stitch length set at 0.

4. To press the seam:

• Press the seam open below the zipper opening.

• On the garment's *left* side, fold and press under the entire 1" seam allowance in the zipper area. Use the clip marking and the end of the zipper opening to position the fold line.

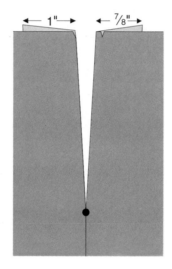

• On the garment's *right* side, press under ⅞" of the 1" seam allowance to create the zipper underlay. (The finished zipper will lap left over right.)

5. To insert the zipper:

• With the right side of the fabric facing upward, position the closed zipper along and under the zipper underlay, with the bottom of the zipper at the base of the zipper opening. Place the underlay fold next to the *right* side of the zipper teeth. Make certain the zipper tab extends above the top of the garment. (With short zippers, it should not be necessary to pin the zipper. Merely "fingerpin" the zipper and stitch.)

• Position your machine's zipper foot to the left of the needle. Stitch next to the fold, from the bottom to the top.

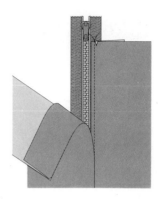

• Lap the garment's *left* side over the garment's *right* side, matching the V-clips. With ½"-wide Sewer's Fix-It Tape or transparent tape, tape the overlap in place.

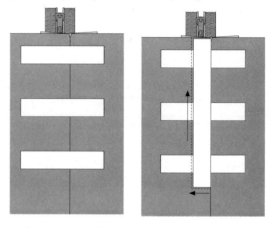

6. To topstitch the lap:

• Align a strip of tape along the folded edge of the lapped seam allowance. This provides an accurate guide for the topstitching line.

• Change the position of the zipper foot so that the foot is to the right of the needle.

• Beginning at the base of the zipper, topstitch along the bottom edge of the tape and up the side.

• Remove the tape.

7. To complete the zipper insertion:

• Move the zipper pull down into the completed zipper placket. Satin-stitch over the ends of the zipper tape at the top of the zipper for reinforcement. Cut off the excess zipper tape.

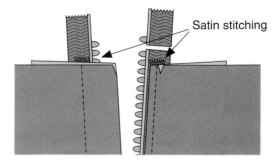

Satin stitching

Mistake-Proof Machine-Sewn Center Zipper

20 Minutes

Sundresses, jumpers, and garments with jewel necklines all have zippered openings at the back neckline. Most sewing directions tell us to insert the zipper, apply the neckline facing, and then handstitch the facing edges in place over the top of the zipper. However, with the following timesaving sewing technique, the facing is completed entirely by machine, minimizing bulk and eliminating all tedious hand sewing.

1. To modify and mark the pattern:

• Trim away ¾" from the center back edge of the neckline facing.

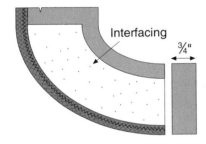

Interfacing

¾"

• Fuse the interfacing to the facing.
• Mark each side of the zipper opening on the garment back, ⅝" from the edge.

2. To stitch the zipper in place:

• Stitch the garment seam from the bottom of the garment to the dot indicating the base of the zipper opening. Press the seam open.

• Fold under the ⅝" seam allowance from the base of the zipper opening to the neckline. Press.

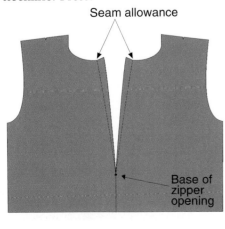

Seam allowance

Base of zipper opening

• Open the zipper and unfold the fabric. With right sides together, align the teeth of the zipper with the pressed crease in the fabric.

Zipper teeth

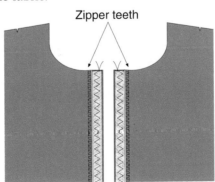

• Zigzag the zipper tape to each seam allowance.

3. To stitch the facing to the neckline:

• With right sides together, align the

Note from Nancy

If your machine does not have a bar-tack setting, drop the machine feed dogs and sew several medium-width zigzag stitches through the facing and seam-allowance layers. With the feed dogs dropped, the fabric will not advance.

Note from Nancy

To prevent a pucker or jamming when starting to sew at a fold, place a multi-layer scrap of fabric under the presser foot. Start sewing on this "anchor cloth" and then feed onto the fashion fabric. When the seam is complete, just clip the anchor cloth away. (Keep it handy for future use.)

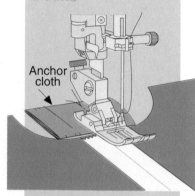

Anchor cloth

facing and garment at the center back opening. Stitch, using a ¼" seam.

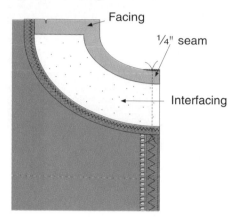

Facing

¼" seam

Interfacing

• Stitch the shoulder seams of the facing. Then stitch the shoulder seams of the garment.

• Align the shoulder seams of the garment and the facing. Pin. At the center-back opening, the garment will wrap around the zipper because the facing was trimmed ¾".

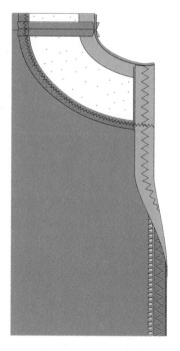

• Stitch the neckline/facing seam.

• Grade the seam allowances and understitch. Turn right side out.

4. To topstitch the zipper in place:

• Close the zipper.

• Press the garment from the right side so that the fabric meets, covering the zipper teeth.

• Center a length of ½"-wide transparent tape over the seam.

• Using the tape as a stitching guide, topstitch the zipper in place. Stitch next to the tape, but not through it.

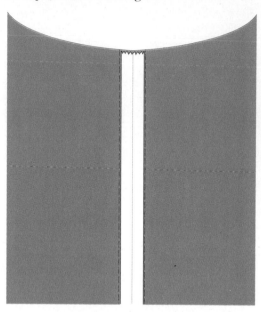

Waistbands Without Bulk

30 Minutes

If you shy away from patterns with separate waistbands because of bulk in the waistline seam, help is on the way. Try this technique, which eliminates much of the bulk by removing part of the seam allowance before the band is cut. Here's how:

1. To cut the band:

• Fold under ½" along the long unnotched edge of the waistband pattern.

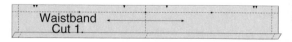

Waistband Cut 1.

• If possible, place the folded edge of the pattern along the selvage edge of the fabric to provide a neat, ravel-free edge. (If it cannot be placed on the selvage, after cutting out you'll need to finish the edge by zigzagging or serging.)

• Cut out the pattern and mark notches and centers.

2. To interface the band:

• Fuse the interfacing to the wrong side of the waistband. Interfacing should not extend into the seam allowances.

• If you are using WaistShaper, position the center slot along the fold line. One side of WaistShaper is ⅛" wider than the other. Position the wider side along the selvage or finished edge of the band and fuse.

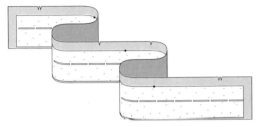

3. To stitch the band:

• With right sides together and notches aligned, stitch the waistband to the garment. The waistband will extend beyond the garment on each end.

• Grade the seam allowances, trimming the waistband seam allowance to ¼" and the garment seam allowance to ⅜".

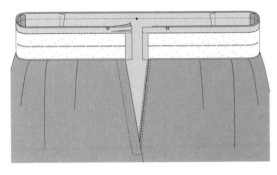

• To reduce waistband bulk even further, cut the garment seam allowances and darts at an angle from the stitching line to the cut edge.

• Cut off any excess zipper tape. Satin-stitch over the ends of the zipper tape to reinforce it.

• Press the seam flat. Then press the waistband up, covering the seam.

4. To stitch the ends of the band:

• With right sides together, fold the band along the center slot, aligning the ends. (The lower edges will not meet; 1 edge will extend ⅛" beyond the other.)

• Stitch ⅝" from the ends. Trim and grade the seam allowances and angle-cut the corners.

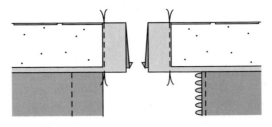

• Turn the waistband right side out. For sharp corners, use a Collar Point & Tube Turner.

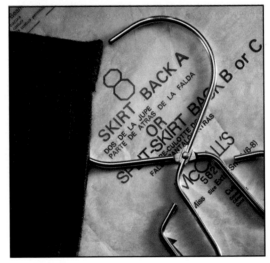

5. To secure the remaining edge of the waistband:

• Pin the back of the waistband to the skirt, covering the waist seam. Pin from the *right* side of the garment. The selvage or finished edge of the band will extend ⅛" below the waistline stitching.

• From the right side of the garment, stitch in-the-ditch of the seam. The ⅛" extension will be caught and secured by the stitching, and the finished band will be perfectly neat and even.

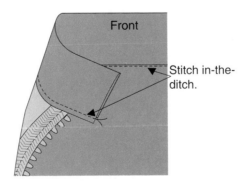

Front

Stitch in-the-ditch.

Timesaving Notions

Use pinking shears to grade and trim seam allowances in 1 step. When you are using lightweight fabrics, trim both seam allowances simultaneously. To minimize bulk when using heavier fabrics, cut each allowance separately.

Timesaving Notions

Pellon Waist-Shaper makes interfacing waist-bands even easier! Available in 1¼" and 2" finished widths, it has perforations along the center that serve as positioning guides. You'll obtain absolutely uniform bands every time!

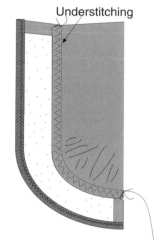

6. Understitch, sewing the seam allowances to the facings with either straightstitch or multi-zigzag.

Understitching

7. To stitch the shoulder or underarm seams:

• Align the stitching lines of the garment front and back pieces exactly where the facings join the garment. Pin together. Matching seams exactly is essential!

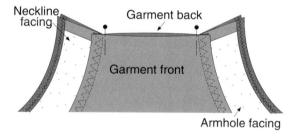

Neckline facing

Garment back

Garment front

Armhole facing

• Stitch continuously, from 1 facing edge to the other facing edge. Because seam angles sometimes vary, it may be necessary to pivot your stitching slightly when you reach the point at which the facing seam meets the shoulder seam.

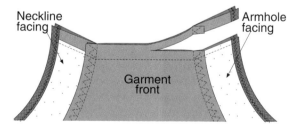

Neckline facing

Armhole facing

Garment front

8. Press the seam allowances flat and then press them open. Within the facing section, trim the seam allowances to ⅜".

9. To tack the facing to the garment:

• Turn the facing to the wrong side of the garment.

Timesaving Notions

Seams Great is a ⅝"-wide nylon tricot strip that neatly binds raw edges without adding bulk. Gently pull Seams Great to determine the curl direction; place the raw edge of the fabric inside the curl. While you are zigzagging it in place, gently pull the Seams Great. It will automatically curl over the raw edge to be finished. (Because Seams Great is made from a low-temperature fiber, avoid touching it with a hot iron.)

Facings Applied Flat

20 Minutes

For a quick and easy facing variation, try sewing the facings to the garment sections before seaming the shoulder lines or armholes. It's so much faster to work in the flat instead of manipulating circles. You can't beat this approach when facing the tiny necklines and armholes found on children's wear.

1. Fuse the interfacing to the wrong sides of the front and back facings.

2. Finish the raw edges of the facings with serging, zigzagging, or Seams Great.

3. Aligning the cut edges and matching notches and markings, stitch the facing to the garment.

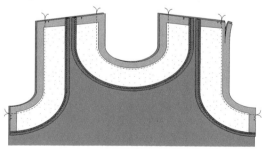

4. Grade the seams, trimming the facing seam allowance to ¼".

5. Press the seams flat and then press toward the facings.

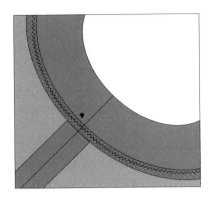

• Place the facing seam allowance and corresponding garment seam allowance under the sewing machine needle. (Be sure the garment is pushed out of the way.)

• Adjust the sewing machine for a zigzag bar tack. Bar-tack through the facing and garment seam allowances only. Do not stitch through the garment.

News in Neckline Facings

—20 Minutes—

Patterns with a back slit opening traditionally suggest stitching the neckline and the slit in 1 operation. How many times have you attempted such an opening and ended up with edges of different lengths? It's a common problem. The next time you use a pattern with a neckline facing, try this updated technique. It gives superior results every time.

1. Fuse interfacing to the wrong side of the neckline facing. Finish the outer edge of the facing.

2. On both the facing and the garment back, mark the cutting line for the back opening with a washable marking pen.

3. With right sides together and matching seam lines and centers, pin the facing to the

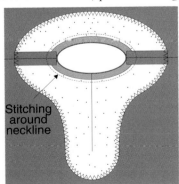

Stitching around neckline

neckline. Stitch around the entire neckline in a continuous seam.

4. Trim and grade the neckline seam allowances, trimming the facing allowance to approximately ¼" and the garment allowance to ⅜".

5. Press all seam allowances toward the facing and understitch.

6. To stitch the back opening:

• Pin the facing to the back opening, aligning the back opening lines. The neckline seam allowances will "wrap" toward the facing side, eliminating bulk at the neckline edge.

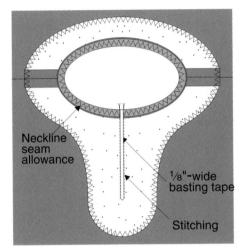

Neckline seam allowance

⅛"-wide basting tape

Stitching

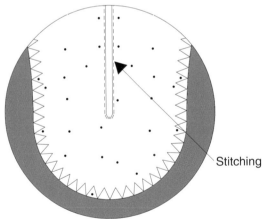

Stitching

• Center a strip of ⅛"-wide basting tape over the stitching line.

• Shorten your stitch length to 12 to 15 stitches per inch. Stitch along both sides of the basting tape, tapering to a point at the end of the opening. Since this area is subject to stress, restitch along both sides of the point for reinforcement.

• Remove the basting tape and cut along the back opening.

• Turn the facing to the inside and press.

Timesaving Notions
Basting tape is commonly used to pin slippery fabrics together. When I sew this facing, I use the narrowest width, ⅛", as a stitching guide. It's difficult to accurately stitch lines that are ⅛" apart; but with this tape, you'll have perfect stitching lines every time.

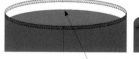

Five
HEMMING SHORTCUTS

Prepressed Hems
—5 Minutes—

Prepress any hem while the fabric lies flat! Then, after the project has been stitched together, you can touch up the prepressed hem to ready it for hand or machine stitching. Try this the next time you're sewing children's sleeves or any area that is difficult to press after it is sewn in a circle.

Stitch Witchery Hem
—10 Minutes—

Stitch Witchery works like a charm when you're hemming garments. The trick is to keep the bonding web on the fabric while fusing, and not on the iron. To prevent this messy problem, serge (or zigzag if you don't have a serger) the bonding web to the wrong side of the edge of the hem. Serging secures the bonding web, trims the web and fabric edges evenly, and finishes the edges, all in 1 step. When you apply a heated iron to the right side of the fabric, the hem will be fused precisely, without the danger of exposing the web to the iron.

Stitch Witchery

Stitching over Bulky Seams
—10 Minutes—

When stitching over bulky seams (in jeans and other heavyweight fabrics), it can be difficult to sew smoothly over the seam. The foot tilts upward and stitches unevenly or jams. To solve this common sewing dilemma, roll up a scrap of fabric and, when approaching the bulky seam, place it under the back of the presser foot or try using a Jean-a-ma-jig. This levels the foot and enables you to sew easily over the bulk, without skipping stitches.

Perfect Marked-Tape Pant Measuring
—5 Minutes—

To hem pants, first try them on and place a pin at the desired length. With the creases folded and the inseam and side seam aligned, lay the pants on the ironing board. Lift up 1 leg and measure the inseam from the crotch to the pin. Mark this measurement on your tape measure. You will never again have to try on pants when hemming (unless you change your mind about length or your size changes). Use your marked tape for a just-right length, every time.

Quick Pattern-Number Reference
5 Minutes

Before you hem a garment, stitch the pattern number in the hem allowance. Try those seldom-used monogram stitches on your sewing machine. Or use a laundry marking pen and write the number directly on the fabric. Then, when someone compliments you on your outfit and asks what pattern number it is, you can simply look inside the jacket, or flip up the hem of your skirt, and presto—you're always ready with the right answer.

Finishing TOUCHES

Dependable Buttonhole Patterns
10 Minutes

Because machine buttonholes are one of the last construction details added to a garment, the buttonhole placement markings you transferred to the fabric when you cut out the garment may disappear by the time they are needed. To avoid remarking the project, make a buttonhole pattern at the time you cut out the garment.

Make the buttonhole pattern out of a temporary stabilizer, such as Wash-Away or Stitch-N-Tear. I recommend that you use this temporary stabilizer over your fabric when you stitch buttonholes, because it provides additional support for light- to medium-weight fabrics. Using this innovative technique, the stabilizer serves 2 purposes: It not only supports the fabric, but it also marks the buttonhole placement.

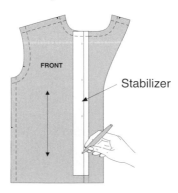

1. Cut a piece of temporary stabilizer 3" wide by the length of the buttonhole area.
2. Place the stabilizer on the pattern, with 1 long edge on the fold line. Mark the stitching line at the neckline edge.
3. Trace the lines for the center front and the buttonhole placement.
4. To stitch the buttonholes:

• Place the stabilizer over the buttonhole area, matching the buttonhole pattern to the fold line and neckline edges. Pin in place.

• Try on the garment. If a buttonhole does not fall at the center of your bust line, move the stabilizer strip up or down. (A buttonhole placed at the bust line will prevent "gaposis.") Repin the strip if necessary to make an adjustment.

• Machine-stitch the buttonholes over the markings on the stabilizer.

• After all the buttonholes are completed, tear away the stabilizer. (If small sections of the Wash-Away remain, simply spritz with water to make them disappear.)

Timesaving Notions
My favorite temporary stabilizer is water-soluble Wash-Away. It's transparent, and it completely dissolves in water in seconds. Incredibly, this thin sheet is strong enough to be stretched in a hoop for stabilizing machine embroidery. And when marking stitching lines on it, you can use an ordinary permanent marking pen.

Serging
THE ULTIMATE TIME-SAVER

The serger sewing machine is the most exciting happening in years! Simply stated, a serger stitches a seam, trims off the excess fabric, and finishes the raw edges, all in one step, and at a speed nearly twice that of a conventional machine. Also called "overlock" machines, sergers are not new to the sewing industry (ready-made garment seams are nearly always serged), but they may be new to you.

A serger will not replace your sewing machine. Rather, it is an accessory that should be used in tandem with a conventional machine, to enhance speed, neatness, and creativity.

With the hope of inspiring you to experiment with your serger, I've compiled essential how-tos and some of my favorite fast-to-serge projects. Enjoy discovering the delights of serging!

AN INTRODUCTION TO
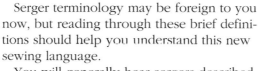
Serging

Note from Nancy

Remember, because the fabric is cut before it is serged, it is essential that you guide the fabric accurately under the foot. (No adjustments can be made at the needle.) Also, for neat, even cutting, make sure that the fabric layers fit in the "mouth" opening.

Serger terminology may be foreign to you now, but reading through these brief definitions should help you understand this new sewing language.

You will generally hear sergers described by the number of threads used on the machine, such as "3-thread," "3/4-thread," "4/2-thread," or "5-thread serger." Some models can be converted to produce additional stitches; for instance, some 3/4- and 5-thread machines have 2-thread capability.

• **Loopers:** Instead of bobbins, sergers have loopers, which loop the threads together in a knit-like fashion.

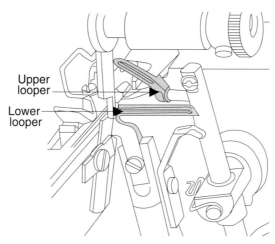

Upper looper

Lower looper

• The upper looper thread is the second (on a 3-thread serger) or third (on a 3/4- or 5-thread serger) thread from the right. This thread does not pass through the fabric; instead, it passes over the surface of the fabric, catching the needle thread on the left and the lower looper thread on the right.

• The lower looper thread is the last thread cone on the right on all but 5-thread sergers. (On 5-thread machines, it is fourth from the right.) Like the upper looper thread, the lower looper thread does not pass through the fabric; instead, it passes underneath the fabric, catching the needle thread on the left and the upper looper thread on the right.

• **Feed dogs:** Sergers have teeth-like grippers, called "feed dogs," nestled in the throat plate. Feed dogs on a serger are nearly twice as long as feed dogs on a sewing machine.

• **Presser foot:** The extra-long presser foot seldom needs to be raised when beginning to serge. Simply lay the fabric on the machine and begin to sew; the fabric will be evenly fed under the foot. In addition to being longer than their counterparts on a conventional sewing machine, most serger feet have a "stitch finger" over which the stitches are formed. Two standard feet are generally included with your serger: 1 with a wider stitch finger for basic overlock seaming and 1 with a narrower stitch finger for narrow-edge serging.

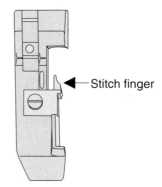

← Stitch finger

• **Blades:** The cutting is done by 2 blades: a stationary blade and a second blade that moves up and down in synchronization with the needle(s). Working together in a jaw-like configuration, the blades "bite" the fabric as you stitch, trimming the seam allowances to ¼".

• **Tension disks or dials:** There is 1 tension disk or drop-in dial for each thread. The tensions usually need at least minor adjustments when changing fabrics, stitches, or threads.

• **Stitch-length dial:** This dial determines the spacing of the stitches. Stitch length on most sergers ranges from about 0.5 mm to 5 mm (from fine satin serging to about 4 to 5 stitches per inch).

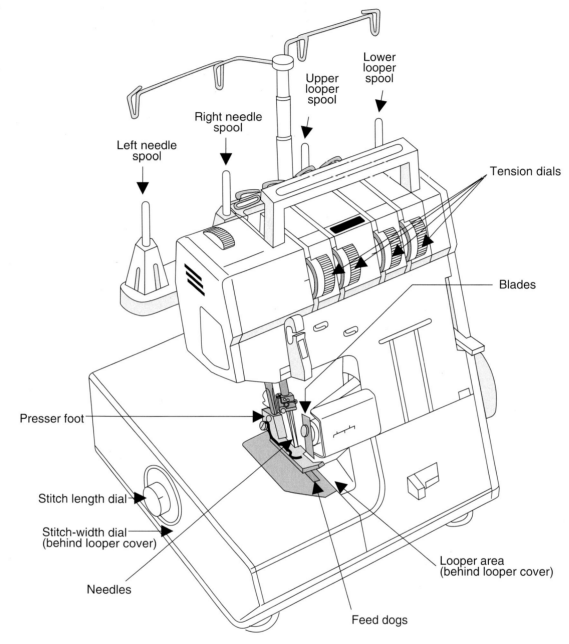

Left needle spool

Right needle spool

Upper looper spool

Lower looper spool

Tension dials

Blades

Presser foot

Stitch length dial

Stitch-width dial (behind looper cover)

Needles

Feed dogs

Looper area (behind looper cover)

Note from Nancy

Refer to your owner's manual for specific information on your serger. The illustration here shows a generic serger. The exact placement of the various parts may be different on your model.

• **Stitch-width dial:** This optional dial is adjacent to the blade area. As the name implies, this dial adjusts the stitch width— the distance between the needle and the blades—also referred to as the "bite." As with other serger measurements, the width is given in millimeters: 0.5 mm to 5 mm (from very narrow to about ³⁄₁₆" to ¼"), with some sergers capable of stitch widths up to 7.5 mm (⅜").

• **Needles:** Although basic 2- and 3-thread sergers have 1 needle, models having 4- or 5-thread capability have 2 needles, as shown at right. One needle or both can be used, depending on the width and type of stitch desired. Take note of the type of needle your serger requires. Although most use regular sewing machine needles (shank with 1 flat side), some require industrial overlock needles (round shank). The industrial needles may be more difficult to find.

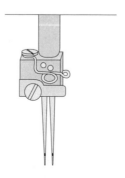

Understanding Basic Serger Stitches

3-thread Overlock

A 3-thread overlock stitch can be produced on a 3-thread, 4-thread, or 5-thread serger. In this stitch, the threads interlock with the needle thread on the left, and the upper and lower looper threads loop together at the fabric's edge. When the looper tensions are balanced, the stitch looks the same on both sides. The 3-thread overlock stitch, generally used for seaming or edge-finishing, is stretchy (ideal for knits) and is very versatile for decorative serging. Try heavier threads, ribbons, or yarns in the loopers.

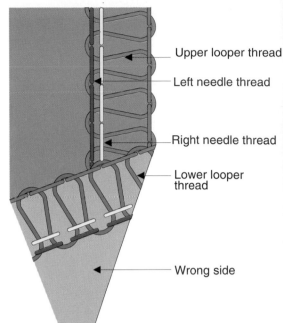

- Upper looper thread
- Left needle thread
- Right needle thread
- Lower looper thread
- Wrong side

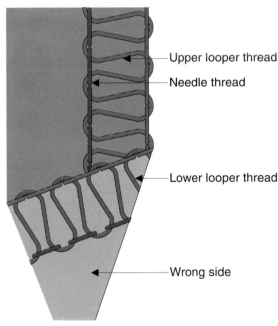

- Upper looper thread
- Needle thread
- Lower looper thread
- Wrong side

3/4- or 4/3-thread Overlock

A 3/4-thread overlock stitch adds a second needle line to the right of the primary seam line. The second line of thread runs through both loopers, creating a stitch that is more stable and durable than the 3-thread stitch.

For specialized serging applications, either needle may be removed. If the right needle is removed, the left needle makes a wider 3-thread stitch. If the left needle is removed, the right needle makes a narrower 3-thread stitch.

With this stitch, intriguing decorative serging is possible.

More Stitch Possibilities

These serger stitches are used for more specialized applications than the basic overlock stitches.

2-thread Overedge

The overedge stitch is formed by thread from 1 needle and 1 looper: the needle and upper looper of a 4/2-, 2/3/4-, or 5-thread serger, or the needle and single looper of a 2-thread serger. An overedge stitch is perfect for finishing edges on lightweight fabrics and for 1-step flatlocking (see page 63), but it must be used in connection with another stitch. Because the upper and lower threads do not lock at the seam line, the overedge stitch cannot be used alone to stitch seams.

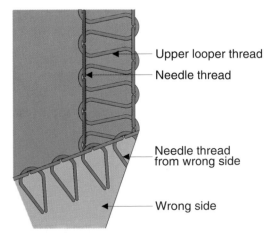

- Upper looper thread
- Needle thread
- Needle thread from wrong side
- Wrong side

2-thread Chain Stitch

On a 4/2-thread serger, the 2-thread chain stitch is formed by thread from the left needle and from the lower looper thread.

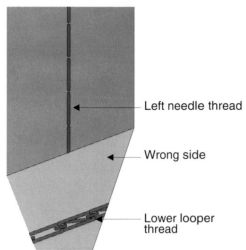

— Left needle thread

— Wrong side

— Lower looper thread

On 5-thread sergers, the stitch is also formed by thread from the left needle and the lower looper thread. On some sergers, the trimming blades can be disengaged and this stitch can be serged anywhere on the fabric, without trimming simultaneously. On other sergers, the chain stitch must be serged along an edge.

For decorative topstitching, especially if heavier or decorative thread is used in the looper, serge with the right side of the project next to the feed dogs.

True 4-thread Stitch

The true 4-thread stitch can only be serged on a machine with 4/2-thread capability, such as a 4/2-serger and most 5-thread sergers. The stitch combines a 2-thread chain stitch and a 2-thread

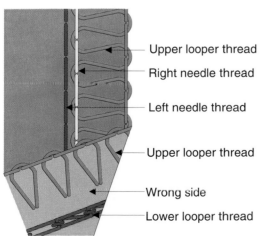

— Upper looper thread

— Right needle thread

— Left needle thread

— Upper looper thread

— Wrong side

— Lower looper thread

overedge stitch, and is best suited for use on woven fabrics or for stabilizing stretchy fabrics.

5-thread Stitch

This is the strongest of all serger seams. Five threads are used at 1 time—2 threads to form the double chain stitch and 3 threads to overlock the edges.

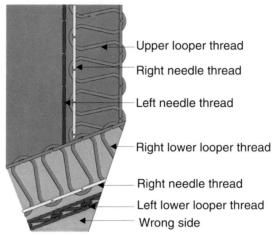

— Upper looper thread

— Right needle thread

— Left needle thread

— Right lower looper thread

— Right needle thread

— Left lower looper thread

— Wrong side

Basic Tension Setting

For most seaming, an overlock stitch should be "balanced." When balanced, the stitch will look the same from the right and wrong sides; the 2 loopers will interlock on the left with the needle thread and on the right, at the fabric edge, with each other. The needle thread should hug the fabric and secure the looper threads without forming loops or causing puckers.

When you receive your serger, the tensions will be set for a balanced overlock stitch. Some brands mark the tension dials or disks with an "N" for normal (balanced).

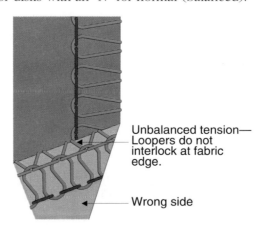

— Unbalanced tension— Loopers do not interlock at fabric edge.

— Wrong side

Note from Nancy

For an easy way to trouble-shoot serger tension problems and to better understand the position of each thread within the stitch, practice with a different-colored thread in each needle and looper. You'll easily see which thread requires tension adjustment. If the overlock is not balanced, begin by loosening the looper that is too tight. Adjust the looper tensions first. If you don't see enough of the thread, loosening is required; if you see too much of the thread (excess loops), tightening is required.

Having difficulty remembering which way to turn your tension dials or disks? My friend, serger expert Gail Brown, relies on the catchy phrase "righty-tighty and lefty-loosey" for tension disks. For drop-in tension dials, remember "up-tight, down-loose." When in doubt, refer to your owner's manual.

On most sewing machines, the upper thread feeds from the side of the spool through the tension guides to the eye of the needle. Ordinary sewing thread, therefore, is wound parallel with the top of the spool. However, the thread path for sergers requires that the thread feed from the top of the spool. For this reason, serger thread is wound in a spiral path, usually on tapered cones, to ease feeding from the top.

Coned serger thread is available in a wide variety of colors. If you have a specific fabric color to match, consider matching only the needle thread (the thread that is visible if the seam is strained). Because the looper threads will not show from the right side of the finished garment, they do not need to match the fabric color exactly.

Decorative Thread— Exciting Options

Try using 1 or all of these specialty threads in your serger to create wonderful decorative effects.

• **Machine embroidery thread** (Sulky, DMC Embroidery Thread, YLI, Dual Duty Plus). Embroidery thread is available in either rayon or cotton. Because this lustrous thread is lightweight, tension adjustment is seldom necessary. These threads are generally sold parallel-wound on traditional spools.

• **Texturized-nylon thread** (Metroflock, Woolly Nylon). This thread is spun, not twisted, and has more stretch than either

Timesaving Notions

If you can't find serger thread to match your fabric color, use regular sewing thread in the needle. Top each thread spool with a serger cap. The cap fits in the top opening of the spool, preventing the thread from catching in the slit in the rim of the spool. Even though this is heavier thread, it will not noticeably increase the weight of the seam because the needle thread stitches in a straight line.

Special Threads for Serging

Coned Serger Thread

In contrast to all-purpose sewing thread, which consists of 3 strands of yarn twisted together (3-ply), serger thread is 2-ply. Because sergers stitch with more threads than conventional sewing machines—usually 3 to 5, depending on the type of seam—they need this lighter-weight thread to reduce bulk at the seam line.

serging or all-purpose thread. Because it is softer than other threads, it is often used when serging lingerie, baby clothes, swimwear, and leotards. Also, because it is not twisted, it is frequently used when increased thread coverage is needed for narrow-rolled and decorative serging. When you use this thread, you may need to loosen the needle or looper tension slightly.

• **Metallic thread.** This lustrous thread beautifully accents dressy garments and accessories. Use it in 1 or both loopers when overlocking, narrow-rolled hemming, or flatlocking seams. Because of the metal content, this thread is a bit wiry and considerably more brittle than ordinary threads. Handle with care when threading loopers and needles, loosening tensions if necessary.

• **Topstitching thread.** This widely available specialty thread works well in the looper(s) of a 3-thread overlock or 2-thread chain stitch. Although some loosening of the tension(s) will be required, I find it to be 1 of the easiest-to-use decorative threads. Look for it on 55-yard spools in a range of fashion colors.

• **Pearl cotton (also available in rayon).** Like topstitching thread, pearl cotton adds a glossy accent when used in the loopers. Because of its popularity for serging, it is now available on cross-wound cones. The most common size is #5 (the bigger the size number, the finer the thread). You may also find pearl cotton sold in skeins for embroidery and crochet. However, the skeins are relatively short (usually less than 10 yards). To use them in your serger, you will have to wind the thread onto an empty cone.

• **Ribbon floss.** For a shiny, 3-dimensional stitch, use this 1/16"-wide mini-ribbon. It is conveniently cross-wound on a 40-yard spool. Use ribbon floss in the looper(s).

• **Decor 6.** This is 1 of the most lustrous decorative threads available for serging. Made of 100% viscose rayon filament, it feeds smoothly through the upper or lower looper guides and eyes. As when using other heavy threads, you must loosen the looper tensions when using Decor 6.

• **ThreadFuse.** A polyester thread twisted with a heat-activated fusible fiber, Thread-Fuse bonds to fabric like magic, with a touch of a steam iron.

Changing Threads— The Fastest Method

Don't rethread your serger from scratch each time you change thread. You'll save time and aggravation by using this tried-and-true tie-on method instead.

Many years ago, I purchased my first serger by mail! I removed it from the box and noticed that the machine was threaded with 3 strands clipped right above the thread rods. Not realizing they were there for a purpose, I proceeded to pull out all 3 threads. Forty-five frustrating minutes later, as I was still trying to thread my serger, I finally read the directions. They began: "Tie the new thread color to the clipped thread tails." Wouldn't that have been easier? Learn from my mistake—don't pull out the thread!

• Clip the existing threads close to the thread cones or spools. Remove the cones or spools from the thread rods.

• Put new cones or spools on the rods and tie the new threads to the existing threads (use slip or square knots). Pull to test the knots, making sure they are secure. If not, retie.

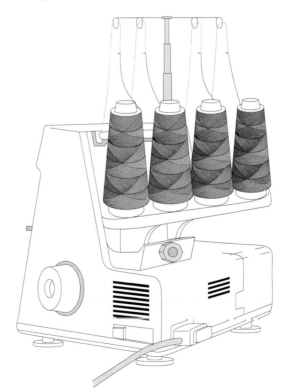

- Trim the thread tails close to the knots.
- Clip the needle thread above the needle eye.
- Turn all tension dials to the loosest settings.
- Chain off a couple of stitches. (The looper threads will separate because you've clipped the needle thread.)

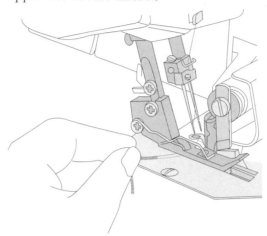

- Pull the looper threads through the machine, gently feeding the knots past the tension guides and dials or disks.
- Pull the needle thread until the knot reaches the eye of the needle. Clip off the knot. Rethread the needle, using serger tweezers if necessary.
- Return the tension dials to the normal (balanced) settings.

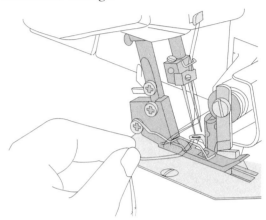

Timesaving Notions

Pattern Pals are pressure-sensitive symbols that make transferring pattern details to fabric very easy. Ideal for marking notches, dots, and circles on seams that will be serged, they eliminate the need for nipped markings that can weaken the seam.

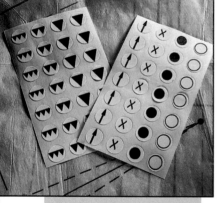

Timesaving Notions

I like to use Flower Head Pins when serging. The flower head lies flat against the fabric, yet is easy to grasp and easy to locate when you are serging a seam. Plus, because the pins are extra long (2"), you use fewer pins for each seam.

Serging
MY FAVORITE
TIMESAVING TECHNIQUES

Fast, Effective Marking

Transfer the pattern markings to the wrong side of the fabric (along the seam line, if possible) with a washable marking pen. Although a common method of marking notches for sewing-machine construction is to make ¼" nip markings into the seam allowance, these markings are not as useful for serger construction. If you cut your garment pieces using standard ⅝" seam allowances, the serger will trim away the nip markings as you stitch. And if you cut the pieces using a ¼" seam allowance, the nip markings will weaken the seam.

Safe Pinning

Place pins parallel to the seam and 1" from the cut edges. Don't pin at right angles to the seam (as you do when stitching on a conventional machine). The serger knives might cut into a pin you forget to remove, dulling or damaging the blades.

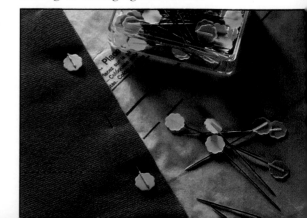

Accurately Gauging Serged Seam Allowances

A serged seam allowance is from ⅛" to
⅜" (3 mm to 10 mm) wide—perfect for
patterns with ¼" seam allowances! But if
your pattern has allowed for ⅝" seams,
align the cut edges of the garment pieces
with the seam-width guide printed on the
looper cover. If your serger does not have
these markings, determine a point ⅝" from
the needle, so that the needle will stitch on
the pattern seam line. Mark this position
with a piece of tape, or use a notion called
a Serger Guide and place it on the looper
cover.

Ravel-Proofing Ends of Seams

Like seams stitched on a sewing machine,
serged seams should be secured at the
beginning and the end. But because a serger
does not backstitch, you'll need to use 1 of
these alternative methods:
• Apply a drop of seam sealant on the
end of the seam. Allow it to dry and clip the
thread tail.
• Use a darning needle or other large-
eyed needle to bury the thread tail under the
looper threads.

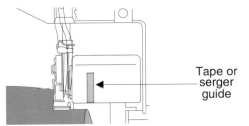

Tape or
serger
guide

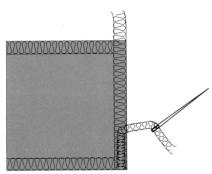

Fast-Serged
30 MINUTE T-SHIRT

A serger can quickly and professionally assemble a rib-trimmed top, T-shirt, or sweatshirt. Rather than sewing the neckline or cuff and ribbing in a circle and then serging the 2 together, the ribbing is applied to the garment flat. Here's how:

1. Adjust your serger for a 3/4-thread or wide 3-thread balanced-tension overlock stitch. Use serger thread in the needle(s) and loopers.

2. Serge 1 shoulder seam with right sides together. Include a piece of Stay-Tape in the seam as you serge. Or fuse a ½" straight-grain strip of interfacing to the wrong side of the back-shoulder seam line before serging.

3. To apply the neckline ribbing:

• Divide the ribbing and the neckline into fourths. Mark the quarter points with pins or a washable marking pen. This is called "quarter-marking."

• Pin the shirt and ribbing together, with right sides together and quarter marks matching.

• Serge the ribbing to the neckline, stretching the ribbing to the shirt. Be careful to align the ribbing ends evenly with the unsewn shoulder-seam edges.

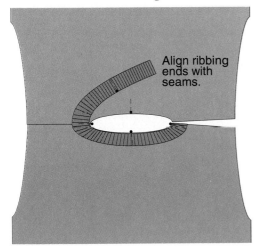

Align ribbing ends with seams.

4. Serge the remaining ribbing and shoulder seam, including the Stay-Tape or interfacing in the shoulder seam. The ribbing ends should match at the neckline edge.

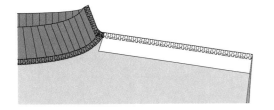

5. Serge the sleeves to the armhole.

6. Apply the cuff ribbing in the manner described in Step 3.

7. Serge 1 side/underarm seam, being careful to match the ribbing edges at the beginning and end of the stitching.

8. Apply the ribbing to the waistline in the manner described in Step 3.

9. Serge the remaining side seam as described in Step 7.

10. Seal all the thread tails with seam sealant. When it dries, clip off the excess thread ends.

Note from Nancy

Some people find that seam ends sealed with Fray Check irritate their sensitive neck skin. Therefore, when I secure the ends of neckline seams, I bury the thread tail instead of applying seam sealant.

Serge a Shirt
(IN LESS TIME
THAN IT TAKES TO SEW ONE)

Serge a shirt, fast! Serged seams, particularly 3/4, 4/2, or 5-thread seams, are durable for both knit and woven fabrics. Contrary to sewers' first assumptions, serging can be used to stitch inside corners, such as collar and lapel areas. The key is "wrapping," a new technique that dramatically enhances the versatility of serging.

Serger "Prep" Work

• Fuse interfacing to the fabric pieces that need to be interfaced. Follow the pattern guide sheet directions.

• Mark notches, dots, and any other necessary markings on the seam lines with a washable marking pen or tailor's chalk.

3. Fold the collar, with right sides together. (The seam allowance should be wrapped toward the under collar.) Serge the ends of the collar. Press the seams flat. Turn the collar right side out. Press.

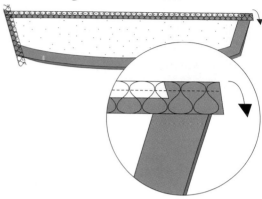

4. Serge the shoulder seams.

5. Pin the underside of the collar to the right side of the garment neckline, matching the notches, dots, and center-back markings.

6. Pin the front facing to the neckline seam with right sides together. (The collar will be sandwiched between the garment and the facing.) Do not pin the center-front edges of the facing and garment together. (If you are working with a shirt front and facing that are a single piece, simply fold right sides together along the fold lines. Sandwich the collar between the garment and facing. Then omit Steps 9 and 10.)

The Best Serging Order

1. Place the under collar and upper collar with right sides together. Serge the outer, unnotched edges.

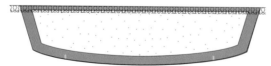

2. Press the serged seam allowance flat and then press it toward the under collar. From the *right* side of the collar, using a conventional straight stitch, understitch the serged seam allowance to the under collar.

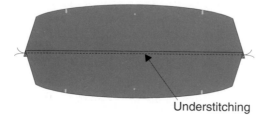

Understitching

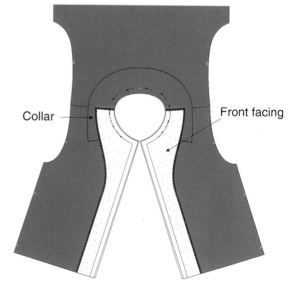

Collar   Front facing

7. Serge the neckline seam.

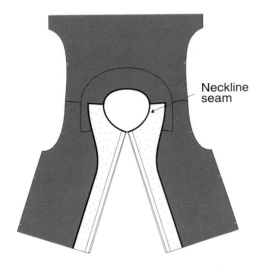

Neckline seam

8. Press the seam flat. Then press the seam allowance to the garment side.

9. Align the garment and front facing, with right sides together. Pin the center front seam, wrapping the neckline seam allowance to the garment side.

10. Serge the center-front seam. Press the seam flat.

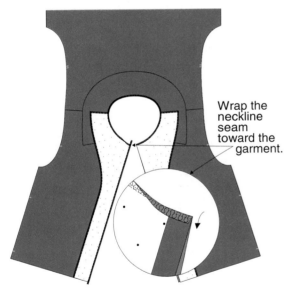

Wrap the neckline seam toward the garment.

11. Turn the facing with right side out, folding along the seam line. Press, aligning the seam line along the edge.

12. Pin the sleeve to the armhole, with right sides together and notches matching. To help

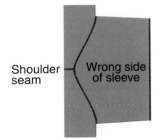

Shoulder seam — Wrong side of sleeve

ease the cap into the armhole, serge with the sleeve side down, next to the feed dogs.

13. Serge to finish the raw edges of the sleeve and bodice hems.

14. Pin the sleeve/side seam with right sides together. Serge the seam in the direction shown.

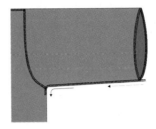

15. Press the hem allowance to the wrong side of the blouse. Topstitch with your conventional sewing machine, using a straight stitch.

16. Stitch the buttonholes using your conventional sewing machine.

Serge-and-Fuse Trim

Try this decorative technique when you are lining a jacket. Serge the facing and lining sections together, using decorative thread in the upper looper (for pipinglike accents) and fusible thread in the lower looper (for assembly speed). Just serge and fuse—the serged seam becomes the decorative "trim."

1. Adjust your serger for decorative/fusible 3/4-thread overlocking. (The right needle line adds needed strength to the seam.)

• Use decorative thread in the upper looper, serger or all-purpose thread in the needles, and fusible thread (such as Thread-Fuse) in the lower looper.

• Set the stitch width at the widest setting.

2. To serge the front-facing/lining seam:

• Press up the hem allowances on the lining pieces.

 Timesaving Notions

ThreadFuse is a polyester thread twisted with a fusible fiber. Use it in the lower looper. Serge with the right side of the fabric up and the fusible thread on the wrong side. After serging a hem edge, simply press the hem to the wrong side of the garment—the Thread-Fuse will fuse the hem in place. When serging a decorative seam as described in the Serge-and-Fuse Trim section, the ThreadFuse creates a fusing strip on the wrong side. In both instances, it is truly a timesaving thread.

Note from Nancy

If fusible thread is not part of your sewing supplies, topstitch the serged seam instead of fusing it. Using matching all-purpose thread in your conventional sewing machine, lap and edgestitch the serged seam to the garment.

• Pin the front lining piece to the front facing, with *wrong* sides together.

• With the facing on top, serge the seam. For accuracy, the left needle line should serge along the ⅝" seam line.

• Press the serged seam allowance toward

the lining. The fusible thread will fuse the seam to the lining. Place an Appliqué Pressing Sheet under the lower part of the facing edge to prevent the fusible thread from fusing to the ironing-board cover.

3. To serge the back-facing/lining seam:

• Pin the back lining to the back-neckline facing, with *wrong* sides together.

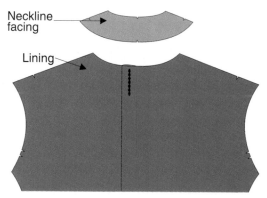

Neckline facing

Lining

• Due to the extreme curve of the back-facing edge, machine-baste first with your conventional sewing machine. Place the facing down, next to the feed dogs, to help ease it to the lining edge.

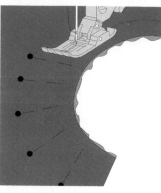

• Serge the facing to the lining with the facing on top. The left needle should stitch along the ⅝" seam line.

• Press the serged seam allowances toward the lining.

• Straightstitch the shoulder seams, with *right* sides together.

Serger Twists—
Timely Accents in No Time!

Add designer detailing with "serger twists." Serge row after row with contrasting-color threads in the upper and lower loopers. Then straightstitch the rows in alternate directions. The serging twists, showing off the different looper thread colors.

1. Adjust the serger for a wide, long 3-thread overlock stitch. (To convert a 3/4-thread stitch, remove the right needle.)

• Use decorative thread—contrasting colors in the upper and lower loopers—to achieve the most dramatic results. The needle thread should be serger or all-purpose thread, in the same shade as the fashion fabric.

• Disengage the blades on the serger, if possible.

• Test the stitch on a scrap of fabric. Adjust the looper tensions (heavier decorative threads require loosening) to achieve a balanced stitch.

2. Prepare the fabric.

• Cut a rectangle of fabric longer than the pattern. Each serger twist takes up an additional ½" to ¾" in length.

• Mark serging lines diagonally or vertically, about 1½" to 2½" apart, using a washable marking pen or tailor's chalk.

3. To serge along the chalk lines:

• Beginning at 1 end of the fabric, fold the fabric with *wrong* sides together along the first line. Serge. *Note:* If the blades cannot be disengaged, guide the fabric away from the blade area.

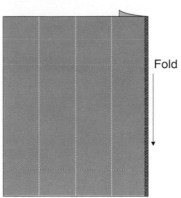

Fold

• Continue serging until all the lines are serged as shown.

4. To mark the straightstitching lines with washable marking pen or tailor's chalk:

• Measure the distance between the serged rows. Use this measurement as the space between the vertical rows.

• Mark the second set of lines at right angles to the lines already serged as shown.

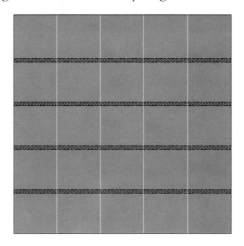

5. To create the "twists":

• Using a conventional sewing machine, straightstitch the first vertical row down over the serged rows.

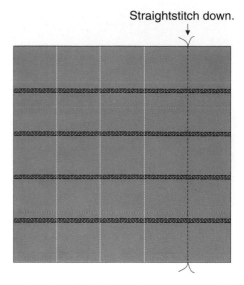

Straightstitch down.

• Straightstitch the next row up, so that the serged seams are twisted, exposing the different-colored threads.

• Continue straightstitching along the marked lines, alternating directions.

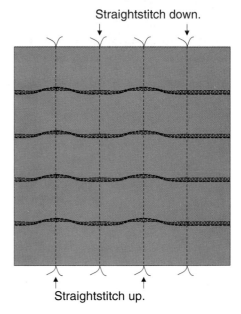

Straightstitch down.

Straightstitch up.

6. Cut the pattern piece out of the serged fabric.

BEYOND SERGER
Basics

Elegant Narrow Rolled Edging

Before the introduction of home-use sergers, only factory workrooms could produce the narrow rolled edges seen on napkins, scarves, and tablecloths. Now, with only a few adjustments, you, too, can serge this lovely, lightweight stitch.

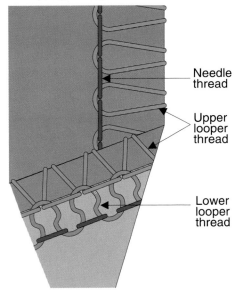

Needle thread

Upper looper thread

Lower looper thread

Easy Adjustments

To create this stitch, a 3-thread overlock or 2-thread overedge stitch is converted to a rolled edge. Tension adjustments are crucial!

Here are general adjustment guidelines for converting to a narrow rolled edge. (Please check your owner's manual for the exact settings for your serger.)

• Replace the standard foot with the narrow rolled-edge foot, which has a narrower stitch finger than the standard foot. On some sergers, the stitch finger is on a separate throat plate instead of on the presser foot; if so, change the throat plate. Other sergers require changing both the foot and the throat plate. A few sergers may require dropping part of the stitch finger

(narrowing the width), instead of changing either the foot or the plate.

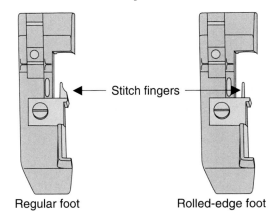

Stitch fingers

Regular foot   Rolled-edge foot

• Narrow the stitch width as much as possible and shorten the setting on the stitch-length dials. Begin with a setting of 2 mm for the stitch length and adjust it as necessary.

• If you are using a 3/4-thread serger, remove the *left* needle.

• You will need to tighten the lower-looper tension *considerably*.

• Test the stitch and adjust the tensions as necessary to achieve the desired look. With the upper-looper tension loosened and the lower-looper tension tightened, the upper-looper thread should roll over the edge.

Rolled-Edge Troubleshooting

Problem: "Pokies"—whiskers of fabric are poking through the rolled edge, especially on the crosswise grain.

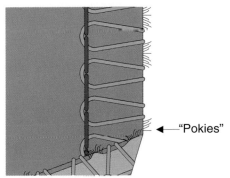

"Pokies"

Note from Nancy

If the tightest lower-looper setting doesn't enhance the rolling action, try "finger tensioning." Place a finger on the lower looper thread (above or below the tension disk or dial) and apply extra pressure. This additional tension usually forces the edge to roll.

Also, don't rule out a narrow "unrolled" edge. For this easy stitch, the narrow stitch finger is used, but the tension remains balanced. I use it when a fabric is particularly resistant to rolling or to expose a lower looper thread that's decorative.

Solution:
• Shorten the stitch length.
• Widen the stitch "bite" (the distance between the blade and the needle). For specific instructions, consult your owner's manual or ask your dealer.
• Use a multifilament thread that spreads over the edge, such as Metroflock or Woolly Nylon.

Problem: The edge doesn't roll to the underside.

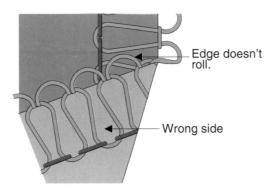

Edge doesn't roll.

Wrong side

Solution:
• Tighten the lower-looper tension.
• Use texturized or monofilament-nylon thread in the lower looper.

Problem: The edge puckers.
Solution:
• Loosen the needle tension. If the looper tension adjustments are straining the needle line, tighten the needle tension.

Problem: The stitch pulls off the fabric.

Solution:
• Lengthen the stitch. The short stitching is too dense for the fabric. (You'll encounter this problem more on lightweight fabrics.)
• Widen the stitch bite. (See your owner's manual.)
• Change the direction in which you are serging.

Narrow Rolled-Edge Options— A "Double" Ruffle

In a matter of minutes, you can serge 2 strips of fabric together to create what looks like a double ruffle. The secret? Seam with a narrow rolled-edge stitch. You can very quickly make yards and yards of 2" trim suitable for use in home decorating, crafts, or children's wear.

1. Adjust your serger for a narrow rolled-edge stitch.
• Use a decorative thread, such as machine embroidery thread, texturized woolly nylon, or metallic thread in the upper looper.
• Use serger or all-purpose thread in a color to match the ruffle fabric in the needle and lower looper.

2. Cut 1 strip of fabric 1½" wide. Cut a second strip from another fabric 3½" wide. (When seamed together, these strips will yield a finished ruffle width of 2".)

3. Place the strips with *wrong* sides together and serge, using the narrow rolled-edge stitch.

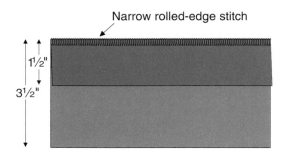

Narrow rolled-edge stitch

1½"

3½"

4. Fold the serged fabric band in half with *wrong* sides together and press. One side will appear to be a double ruffle because of the rolled edge joining the 2 strips.

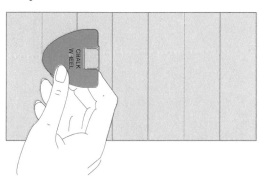

Wrong sides together

5. Straightstitch the ends of the ruffle, with right sides together, forming a circle.

6. Gather the long unfinished edge and apply the ruffle to your project.

Easy, Pretty Pin Tucks

Create delicate pin tucks quickly, using your serger's narrow rolled-edge stitch. Serged pin tucks are perfect for heirloom-look blouses, children's wear, and decorator accessories.

1. Adjust your serger for a medium-to-long narrow rolled-edge stitch. Use machine-embroidery thread in the needle and looper(s).

2. Cut a rectangle of fabric approximately 2" to 3" wider than the pattern piece.

• Mark the pin tuck placement lines vertically on the fabric, using a chalk wheel or a washable marking pen. Lines spaced 1" apart will produce pin tucks approximately ¾" apart.

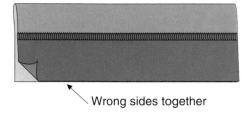

• Fold along the marked lines, with *wrong* sides together.

3. Disengage the cutting blades, if possible. If not, be sure to guide the fabric just slightly to the left of the blade so that it is not accidentally cut. Serge along each fold. Presto—instant pin tucks!

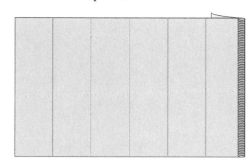

Note from Nancy

To make the most elegant serger pin tucks, use a decorative thread in the upper looper.

Note from Nancy

I usually recommend that the interfacing extend ⅛" into the seam allowance, so that it is secured by machine stitching. However, since this blouse's outer edges are exposed, it is wise to trim the interfacing to the seam line. Trimming this way will prevent any interfacing from showing at the exposed edge.

A Quick-Serged Blouse

Use the narrow rolled-edge stitch to serge blouses made of light-to-medium-weight fabrics. The quick-serged edge is perfect for jewel-neckline tops or even a blouse with a collar and lapel detailing. The serging is exposed along the stitched edge, resulting in a finish that is decorative and free of bulk. Here are the steps:

1. Trim away the interfacing seam allowances and fuse interfacing to the wrong sides of the front and back facings.

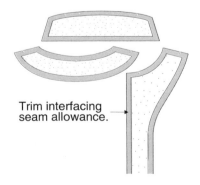

Trim interfacing seam allowance.

2. To adjust your serger for a narrow rolled-edge stitch:

• Use specialty thread in the upper looper. In the lower looper and needle, use matching serger or all-purpose thread.

• Test the stitch on a scrap of fabric. Adjust the tensions and length if necessary for better thread coverage.

3. To serge the collar:

• Place the collar pieces with *wrong* sides together, with the upper collar on top.

• Serge the unnotched edge of the collar. The rolled-edge stitch is most attractive from the top side. The needle should stitch along the ⅝" seam line.

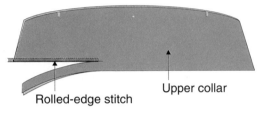

Rolled-edge stitch   Upper collar

• Serge the ends of the collar with the upper collar on top.

Serged end

• Place a drop of seam sealant on the thread tails at the edge of the fabric at the collar corners. After the sealant dries, carefully clip off the excess tails.

4. Place the front and back pieces with *right* sides together at the shoulder seams. Serge the shoulder seams. (This serged edge *will not* be exposed.)

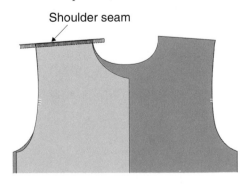

Shoulder seam

5. To serge the front facing:

• Pin the facing to the garment front with *wrong* sides together.

• With the facing on top so that the

attractive side of the rolled-edge stitch will be exposed, serge the center-front edge to the facing. The serger will trim the seam allowances as you serge.

• Align the needle line with the seam line.

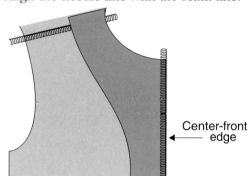

Center-front edge

6. To serge the neckline and collar:

• Pin the *right* side of the collar to the *wrong* side of the neckline, matching notches and circles.

• Serge the collar to the neckline, with

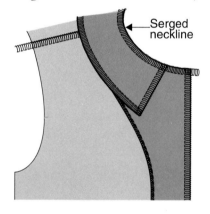

Serged neckline

the collar piece on top. The collar must be on top to have the attractive side of the rolled-edge stitch exposed.

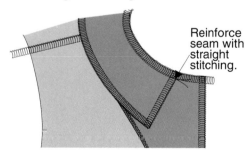

Reinforce seam with straight stitching.

• With conventional straight stitching, reinforce the seam line where the collar and neckline meet.

• Secure the thread tails with seam sealant. Clip off the excess thread.

7. Finish the blouse by seaming the sides and sleeves with right sides together. Turn the blouse right side out.

Decorative, Functional Flatlocking

Just about any serger can flatlock—all you need is 3-thread or 2-thread stitch capability. After making tension adjustments, simply serge 2 layers together and then pull them apart until the fabric is flat. The result? A stitch that is versatile for both decorative seaming and "topstitching."

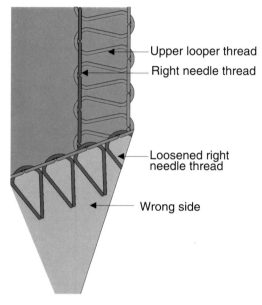

Upper looper thread

Right needle thread

Loosened right needle thread

Wrong side

Easy Adjustments

Check your owner's manual or workbook for specific recommendations. Here are the general guidelines for 3-thread flatlocking:

• If seaming, pre-trim excess allowances. Although it's best to test the width of the flatlock seam on scraps, you can estimate that the seam will be about ¼" (5 mm to 6 mm).

• If "topstitching" with flatlocking (on a fold), fold the fabric with wrong sides together along the line you want to embellish.

• Use the standard presser foot and stitch finger.

• Loosen the needle tension to "0" or as much as possible.

• Tighten the lower looper by 4 to 5 settings.

• Leave the upper looper at the normal tension setting.

• Guide the fabric away from the blade.

• Use only the *left* needle of a 3/4-thread or 5-thread serger; this will give the widest flatlock stitch.

Note from Nancy

Use the quick-serged edge to finish a softly curved neckline and armholes. Place the wrong side of the facing on the wrong side of the top. Then serge! Again, for accuracy, align the needle line with the seam line.

Note from Nancy

If you have a serger with 2-thread overedge capability, such as a 2/3/4-thread, some 5-thread, and some late model 2-thread machines, flatlocking usually requires no tension adjustments at all. Serge the fold or edge, pull flat, and voila!—it's flatlocked. However, when you are using heavier fabrics or threads, it may be necessary to loosen both the needle and looper tension.

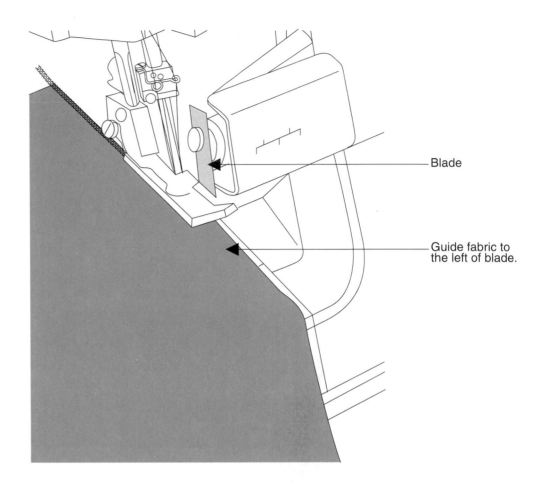

Blade

Guide fabric to
the left of blade.

Note from Nancy

*To serge the best flatlock
stitch, the lower-looper
thread should be tightened
to form a straight line. In
addition to adjusting the
tension dials, another way
to tighten the lower-looper
thread is to use texturized
Woolly Nylon thread. This
thread stretches as it passes
through the guides, increas-
ing the tightening action.
Another alternative is to use
"finger tensioning."*

• Test the stitch on a scrap of fabric. For
the flattest flatlocking, guide the fabric to
the left of the blade, so that the stitches
hang over the edge slightly. (Doing this
allows space for the fabric under the stitch
and prevents the problem of accidentally
cutting the fabric if you are flatlocking a
fold.)

• Grasp the fabric on both sides of the
stitches and gently pull to flatten.

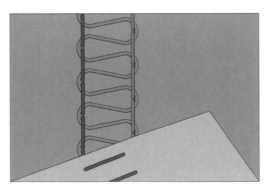

Flatlock Troubleshooting

Problem: The stitching doesn't pull completely flat.

Doesn't pull flat.

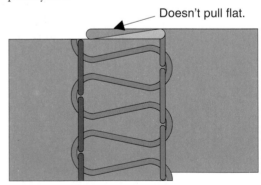

Solution:

• Loosen the needle tension.

• If you've loosened it as much as possible, remove the needle thread from the
tension disk or dial.

• If your serger has drop-in tension dials,
cover the tension slot with a piece of transparent tape. Or, if your machine has knob-
type dials, do not engage the thread in the
dial.

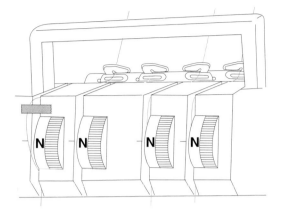

• When flatlocking, allow the stitches to hang over the edge slightly.

Decorative Possibilities— Flatlocking Fun!

By simply changing the thread types and colors combined in the stitch, many different flatlock looks can be created.

• **"Framed" loops.** Use contrasting-colored threads in the needle and lower looper to frame the upper-looper thread.

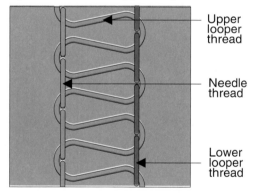

Upper looper thread

Needle thread

Lower looper thread

• **"Floating" loops.** Use "invisible" monofilament thread in the needle and lower looper. For the upper looper, use decorative thread; the upper-looper thread will appear to float on top of the fabric.

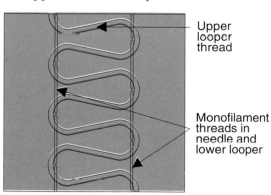

Upper looper thread

Monofilament threads in needle and lower looper

"Ladder" stitch. Use topstitching thread in the needle. To accommodate the thicker thread, also change to a larger-size needle. For the upper and lower loopers, use serger thread. Serge with wrong sides together so that the ladder stitch will appear on the top of the fabric.

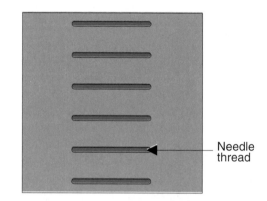

Needle thread

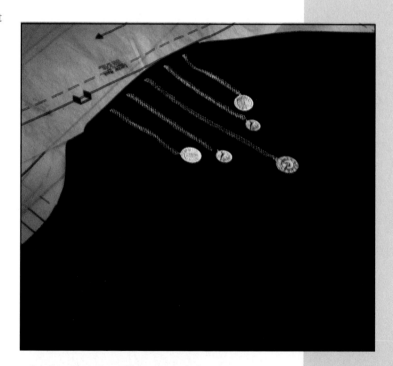

Flatlocked "Topstitching"

Flatlocked "topstitching" adds interesting texture and color to any fabric. It's easiest to flatlock evenly and uniformly when the fabric is flat, before the project is seamed. Here's how:

1. Adjust your serger for a flatlock stitch.
• Use decorative thread in the upper looper of a 3-thread stitch and the looper of a 2-thread stitch.
• Use matching all-purpose, serger, or clear monofilament thread in the needle.

(For 3-thread flatlocking, also use 1 of the same threads in the lower looper.)

2. Cut out the pattern. Mark the fabric with a linear design, using a washable marking pen, chalk wheel, or tailor's chalk.

3. To "topstitch" fabric with flatlocking:

• Fold *wrong* sides together along 1 of the lines marked on the fabric.

• Disengage the blades, if possible.

• Place the fabric underneath the presser foot, positioning the fold just to the left of the blade "mouth." (The stitches will hang off the edge slightly.)

• Flatlock the fold.

• Gently pull the fabric flat.

4. Continue flatlocking along all the marked lines.

From Ribbon to Fabric— Flatlock Your Own

Create your own fabric by flatlocking ribbons and/or lace together into an eye-catching piece of fabric art.

1. Adjust your serger for a flatlock stitch.

• Try floating-loop flatlocking for an unusual effect.

• Optional: Use decorative thread in the looper of a 2-thread stitch or in the upper looper of a 3-thread stitch.

• Use matching all-purpose, serger, or clear monofilament thread in the needle. (For 3-thread flatlocking, also use 1 of the same threads in the lower looper.)

2. To flatlock the ribbons and/or lace together:

• Place the ribbons with wrong sides together.

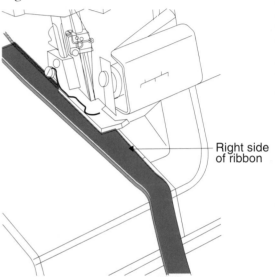

Right side
of ribbon

- Disengage the blades, if possible.
- Place the ribbons under the presser foot, guiding them just to the left of the blade "mouth."
- Gently pull the ribbons flat.

3. Continue flatlocking the ribbon and/or lace together until the fabric is large enough for your project or pattern piece.

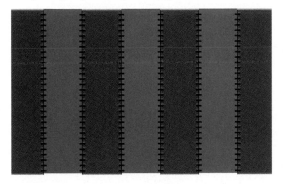

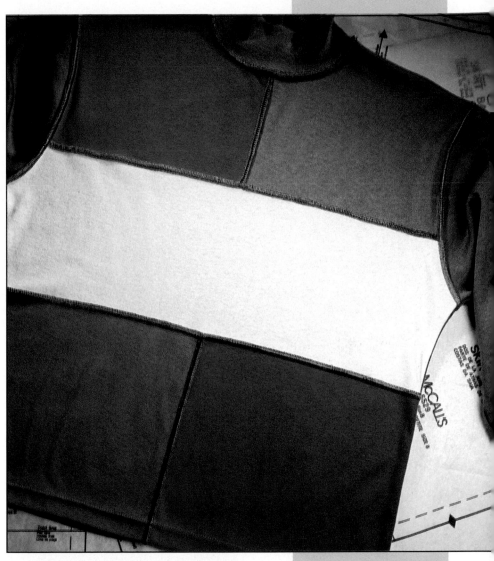

Twice-Stitched Seam— Straight Stitching + Flatlocking

Why not flatlock over a conventionally sewn seam? The twice-stitched seam is not only decorative, but stronger than the seam that is only flatlocked. For a creative combination, use flatlocked seams with color blocking (see photo at right).

1. Straightstitch the ⅝" seam on your conventional sewing machine.

- Press the seam flat and then open. This 2-step pressing technique forms a neat fold along the seam, making the seam easier to flatlock.

2. To flatlock the straightstitched seam:

- Fold along the seam, with *wrong* sides together.
- Adjust the serger for flatlocking, using a decorative thread in the looper of a 2-thread or the upper looper of a 3-thread.
- Place the seam under the serger presser foot, guiding the fold just to the left of the blade "mouth."
- Gently pull the seam flat. Press the seam if necessary.

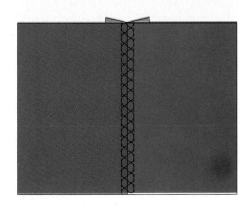

SUPER-QUICK *Knits*

Which are your most comfortable clothes? For me, comfort is synonymous with my wardrobe favorites, all of which are knits: a fleece jumpsuit, a wool-jersey dress, and a pair of interlock pants. Undoubtedly, comfort ranks as the outstanding virtue of knits, but another advantage is easy fit. If, like many of us, your figure fluctuates at times, knit fabrics can expand to fit, camouflaging the changes.

Knits also mean super-fast construction when you are sewing. Whether you sew on a 20-year-old Singer, the newest high-tech computer machine, or a serger, knit garments can be completed in minutes.

Note from Nancy

You'll find a wide range in the price and quality of knits at fabric stores. The bargain-priced knits are the most tempting to buy. But remember, although it takes the same amount of time to sew quality fabric as it does bargain fabric, the first-quality fabrics usually last longer. My advice—buy the best quality you can afford. In the long run, it's economical as well as timesaving.

Knits: HOW ARE THEY DIFFERENT?

Interlocks

Knit fabrics are created by interlocking loops of yarn. Interlock knits are constructed with 2 loops of yarn (1 loop knit from the back and 1 from the front of the fabric) and are classed as double-knit fabrics. Like other double knits, interlock looks the same on the right and wrong sides. (Don't be confused by the term "double knit." During the 1970s, it was synonymous with the stable, plastic-like, 100%-polyester fabric.) Today's interlock double-knit fabrics, made of cotton- or cotton-and-polyester yarns, are lightweight, drapable, comfortably soft, and stretchable.

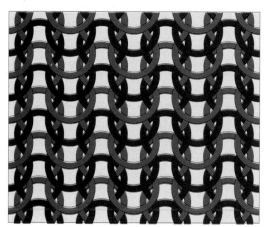

For many sewers, the most desirable interlock is 100% cotton. Although 100%-cotton interlock can be more expensive and may shrink more than cotton/polyester blends, it is less clingy and less prone to pilling. On the other hand, interlock blends of 50% cotton/50% polyester are more affordable, shrink less, and are sold in a wider assortment of colors than the all-cotton variety.

Pretreating Interlocks

Pretreat washable interlocks by laundering the fabric as you will the finished garment. For best results, pretreat any 100%-cotton interlock by washing and drying it twice. This double washing eliminates any residual shrinkage and also compacts the yarns, adding body to the finished garment.

Jersey

A jersey is a single-knit fabric, formed from 1 set of yarn loops–smooth on the right side, with horizontal loops running crosswise on the wrong side. Because the yarn loops are often very fine, it may be difficult to tell the difference between the 2 sides. To determine the right side of a jersey knit, hold a cut edge–either cross-grain or selvage–and pull to stretch the edge. A jersey will always roll to the right side.

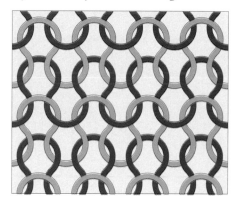

Look for jersey fabrics in a variety of fibers, such as acrylic, wool, cotton, or blends. The wool and wool-like (acrylic) jerseys have the greatest body and least tendency to roll or curl. Cottons and cotton/polyester-blend jerseys are lighter in weight; they are well suited to use in T-shirts and children's wear but are generally too limp for use in dresses or skirts. Blends of cotton and Lycra (usually 10% to 15% Lycra) are perfect for stretch pants and active wear.

Pretreating Jerseys

To pretreat any washable jersey, machine-launder the fabric as you will handle the finished garment. If the fabric is 80% or more cotton, look for possible shrinkage of up to 10%.

When you are using wool jersey, have it steamed by a dry cleaner. Steaming preshrinks the fabric and removes surface sizing.

Determining the Stretch Percentage of Your Knit

Not all knits stretch the same amount. The fiber content and type of knit construction dictate the amount of stretch.

Look for a stretch gauge on the back of your pattern envelope. This gives you a way to test the stretch of the fabric at the store. (Some patterns state the amount of stretch required by the pattern, such as "25% stretch" or "50% stretch.")

To quickly determine the amount of stretch of a knit fabric:

1. Fold under 3" along the cut edge of the fabric (the cross-grain) to prevent the cut edge from stretching excessively during the test.

2. Measure 10" of the fabric and see how far it stretches:

    10" stretches to 12½" = 25% stretch
    10" stretches to 15" = 50% stretch

Laying Out and Cutting Knits

Even after your knit fabric has been pretreated, the center fold line may remain permanently set, resulting in a line that is too conspicuous. Refold the fabric to cut around this line. For jerseys and other flat knits, bring the selvage edges to the original fold line, creating 2 new fold lines, 1 on each side. For interlocks, which are usually knit in a tube, roll the tube so that the permanent fold lines do not lie at the edges of the fabric.

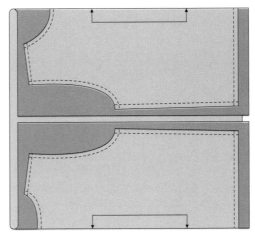

Also remember that the one-way formation of the interlocking loops creates a difference in shading on knit fabrics similar to the nap found on velvet or corduroy. Because of this one-way shading, you will need to use the "one-way" layout when you are positioning and cutting your garment pieces. Check the pattern envelope to make sure you buy the proper amount of fabric.

Note from Nancy

The right and wrong sides of interlock knits look the same and can be used interchangeably, unless you're using an interlock print, of course. One caution: To avoid confusion, mark 1 side as the wrong side with a washable marking pen or transparent tape. Otherwise, you may end up with 2 right sleeves and no left sleeve!

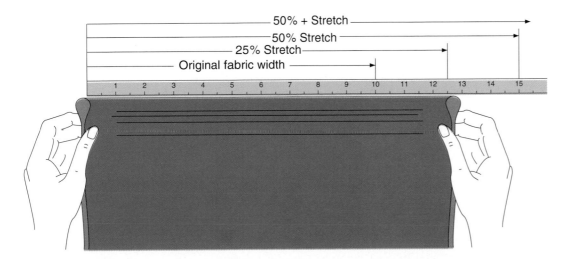

Note from Nancy

In the past when using a double needle, I would guide 1 thread to the left of the tension disk and the other thread to the right of the disk. At times my double needle stitching wasn't balanced. After experimenting with threading both threads through the same tension disk, I found the thread tensions were more balanced! From now on, take this simpler and faster approach when using a double needle.

THE *Basics:* SIMPLE-TO-SEW KNIT SEAMS

Machine-Stitched Seams

If you sew without a serger, don't despair. Your conventional zigzag machine has several stitches that can be used as functional, fashionable seaming alternatives.

Traditional Knit Seams

For best results when you sew with knits, always use Stretch, Yellow Band, or ballpoint needles. If you have worked with knit fabrics before, you may have noticed tiny holes that form along the seam line or topstitching line. The holes are caused by the acute points of "sharp" sewing machine needles, which pierce the yarn fibers. The Stretch, Yellow Band, or ballpoint needles have rounded points that slip between the fine knit loops and do not cause holes.

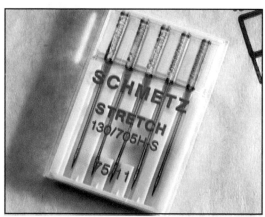

To produce a neat seam on knit fabric:
1. Straightstitch along the seam line. Or, to provide additional stretch in the seam, use a narrow zigzag stitch along the seam line.
2. Using a medium-width, medium-length stitch, zigzag the seam allowances together, close to the seam line.
3. Trim away the excess seam allowance close to the zigzag stitches.

Double-Needle Seams and Hems

Another way to add stretch to seams on knit fabric is to stitch with a double needle. The 2 top threads pass through the twin needles, creating 2 straight lines of stitching on the top of the fabric, while the bobbin thread zigzags back and forth between the needle threads. Although the double-needle stitch is usually used for hemming and decorative topstitching, it also builds flexibility into knit seams.

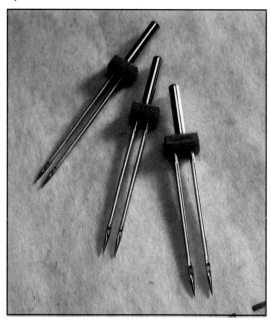

To stitch a double-needle seam:
1. Use 1 spool of thread on each of the spool pins on top of the machine.
• If your sewing machine has only 1 spool pin, wind extra bobbins and stack the bobbins on the spool pin instead of using a spool of thread.
• Following the threading instructions for your machine, guide both threads as 1 through the tension disk and thread guides. At the needle area, separate the threads and thread each needle with 1 thread.

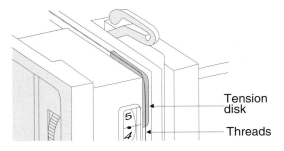

Tension
disk

Threads

2. To ensure an accurate ⅝" seam, change the needle position so that the left needle lines up with the center of the presser foot. If the needle position cannot be changed, adjust the ⅝" seam guideline so that the left needle stitches along the ⅝" seam line.

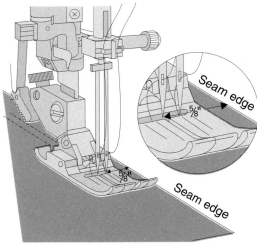

Seam edge

⅝"

⅝"

Seam edge

3. Stitch the entire garment using a 2-mm, 3-mm, or 4-mm double needle.

4. Press the seams to 1 side, with the zigzagging down. Because of the formation of the stitches, the seams will automatically lap with the double stitching on top.

To stitch a double-needle hem, press under the hem allowance. Stitch along the hem edge, from the right side, with the double needle.

Topstitched Seam

To create a designer-style topstitched seam:

1. Straightstitch a normal ⅝" seam, using a single needle. Press (or finger-press) the seam open.

2. On the right side of the garment, topstitch ⅜" from each side of the seam line, using a medium-length straight stitch (10 to 12 stitches per inch) or a medium-width, medium-length zigzag stitch.

Topstitched Hem

To create a fast and easy topstitched hem, press under the hem allowance. Topstitch from the right side, using either a straight or zigzag stitch.

Topstitched Facingless Edges

Consider eliminating the neckline and armhole facings when you are sewing with knit fabrics. This ready-to-wear technique of turning and topstitching speeds up construction, cuts down on facing bulk, and finishes edges beautifully. Because knit fabrics don't ravel, there is no need to finish the raw edges on the wrong side.

To create a topstitched edge:

1. Eliminate the facing piece(s). Press under the seam allowances.

2. Straightstitch or zigzag ½" from the fabric fold. You're finished!

Note from Nancy

"Finger-press" simply means to apply pressure to the seam by compressing the fabric layers between your thumb and index finger. On knit fabrics, it is a fast and effective way to "press" seams quickly.

Serged Seams

In ready-to-wear clothing, serged seams are the norm. Look inside purchased T-shirts, sweats, or knit tops. Notice how neat the seaming appears: Serging trims off the excess seam allowance and stitches the 2 pieces together while overlocking the edge. Now, with home sergers, you can serge knit garments literally in minutes, without sacrificing construction quality.

To serge seams on knit fabrics, use a 3- or 3/4-thread overlock stitch adjusted for balanced tension. (Refer to Chapter 3 for more details on serging.) Unless color matching is critical, use all-purpose serger thread in the needle and both loopers.

Check ready-made clothing for construction ideas. Even the most expensive lines of designer clothing feature topstitched seams and other details that add seam line accents and stability while reducing pressing time.

Serge It Decoratively

Try using decorative threads in the looper(s) and then purposely exposing the seam. (Add a few minutes to your sewing time for testing the decorative serging technique on scraps of your fabric.)

Decoratively Serged Seams

To make a decoratively serged seam:

1. Serge, with *wrong* sides together, along the ⅝" seam line. (The blades will trim the excess seam allowance while serging.)

2. Use a medium-to-wide stitch width, short stitch length, and decorative thread in the upper looper. Try using Woolly Nylon or Metroflock (both texturized nylon threads) or Decor 6 (a rayon topstitching thread) in the upper looper. (For more decorative thread possibilities, see Chapter 3.)

- Serge the seam so that the decorative serging will show.
- Finger-press the seam to 1 side.
- Using a conventional sewing machine, edgestitch the seam to the fabric.

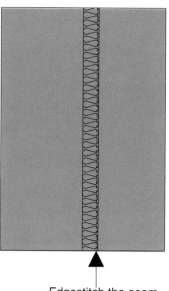

Edgestitch the seam.

Decoratively Serged Hem

If you have decoratively serged the seams, consider unifying the garment's design elements by decoratively serging the hem.

To make a decoratively serged hem:

1. Use a medium-to-wide stitch width, short stitch length, and decorative thread in the upper looper. With the *wrong* side of the garment facing up, serge along the edge of the hem. (You will be serging a single layer of fabric.) Allow the serger blades to trim the edge of the hem slightly; a more uniform stitch can be produced in this way.

2. Press the hem to the *right* side, exposing the decorative serging. With a conventional sewing machine, edgestitch along the serged needle line to complete the hem.

Note from Nancy

Because the wrong side of the hem allowance shows on the right side of the garment, decoratively serged hems can be used only on reversible interlock knits. So when you are using jersey or any other knit with definite right and wrong sides, avoid this hem treatment.

Organize
QUICK-KNIT SEWING BASICS INTO TIME UNITS

Stabilize Stress Areas
— *10 Minutes* —

With fusible interfacing, it takes only a few minutes to stabilize your knit garment in areas that easily sag or stretch out of shape.

To stabilize pants:
• Fuse interfacing to the wrong side of the fabric in the knee area, from 4" above to 4" below the stress point, to prevent sagging.

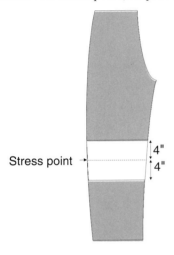

Stress point | 4" / 4"

• Fuse a ¾"-wide bias strip to the wrong side of the pocket, even with the cut edge, to prevent stretching.

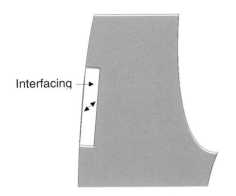

Interfacing →

To stabilize shirts and tops:
• Fuse a ¾"-wide strip of interfacing, cut on the lengthwise grain, to the shoulder seams on the front garment pieces only.

Interfacing

Special Zipper Application for Knits
— *20 Minutes* —

In the past, I found that zippers in knit garments tended to ripple and buckle, so I avoided them altogether. But now, with the help of fusible-tricot interfacing (such as Easy Knit) and a paper-backed fusible web (such as Wonder-Under), putting a zipper in a knit jumpsuit or jumper is a simple 20-minute process.

Purchase a nylon or polyester zipper that is 1" to 2" longer than the opening. The extra length allows you to slide the zipper tab away from the presser foot and avoid crooked stitching. (The excess length will be trimmed off in Step 8.)

To insert the zipper:

1. Cut 2 (1¼"-wide) strips of fusible-tricot knit on the lengthwise grain and fuse them

Note from Nancy

To save time later, cut several ¾" to 1"-wide Easy Knit strips now. Using your shears or a rotary cutter, cut some on the lengthwise grain and others on the bias.

Timesaving Notions

Sewer's Fix-it Tape is a terrific tape to use when topstitching zippers. Like transparent tape, it is ¹/₂" wide, yet it is much softer and easier to handle. Use it also for altering patterns. The tape can even be repositioned without tearing the tissue pattern.

to the wrong side of the zipper area. This lightweight interfacing will stabilize the zipper area, preventing the knit fabric from rippling as the zipper is inserted.

2. Machine-baste the zipper opening closed. Press the seam open.

3. Cut 2 (¹/₂"-wide) strips of paper-backed fusible web. Fuse the strips to the *wrong* side of the seam allowances. Peel off the paper backing. Fuse the seam allowances to the wrong side of the garment pieces by pressing the seam open again.

4. Cut 2 more ¹/₂"-wide strips of fusible web the length of the zipper tape. Fuse the strips to the *right* side of the zipper tape. Peel off the paper backing.

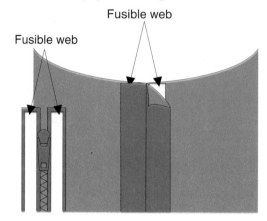

Fusible web

Fusible web

5. Center the zipper face down over the seam, extending the extra zipper length above the fabric. Press to fuse the zipper in place.

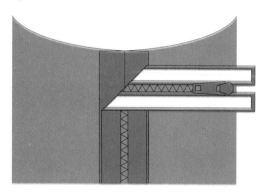

6. Turn the garment right side out. Center a length of ¹/₂"-wide transparent tape or Sewer's Fix-it Tape over the seam line. On each side of the seam line, stitch from the bottom to the top of the zipper, using the tape edge as a stitching guideline.

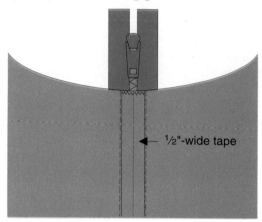

← ¹/₂"-wide tape

7. Remove the transparent tape. Open the basting stitches.

8. Open the zipper. Bar-tack across the top on each side of the zipper. Trim the excess zipper length even with the seam allowance.

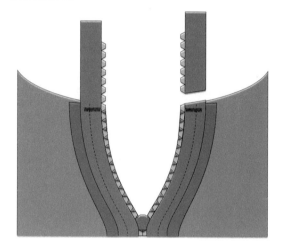

Crossover Mock Turtleneck

20 Minutes

You've seen this clever crossover neckline in catalogs and stores everywhere–on men's, women's, and kids' T-shirts and sweatshirts. The crossover neckline is much easier to sew than you would imagine, and it provides another option for customizing basic sportswear tops.

To make the crossover turtleneck:

1. Purchase ribbing in a color to match or contrast with your shirt fabric.

2. Cut the ribbing 3" to 6" wide by the length of the ribbing pattern plus 3" for an overlap.

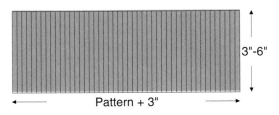

3"-6"

Pattern + 3"

3. Fold the ribbing in half lengthwise, with wrong sides together.

4. Measure in 3" from each end along the cut edge; mark. Trim the ends at an angle, beginning at the 3" mark and tapering to the fold.

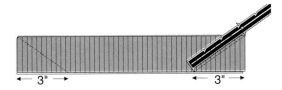

3"   3"

5. Overlap the ribbing ends by 3", aligning the cut edges at the bottom. Machine-baste or serge the edges together, rounding off corners.

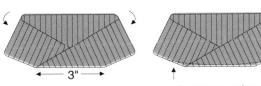

3"

Baste cut edges together around corners.

6. Quarter-mark the ribbing and garment neckline as shown. Align the quarter markings, with right sides together. Pin, centering

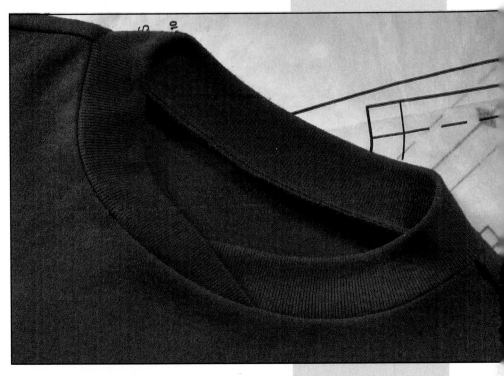

the overlapped ribbing at the center front of the garment.

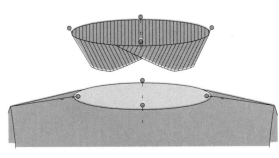

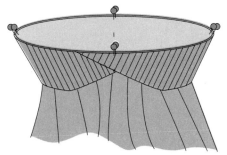

7. Serge or sew the ribbing to the neckline, stretching the ribbing to fit.

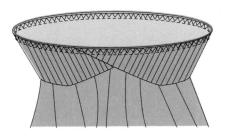

Note from Nancy

To make certain that the center front of the ribbing always lines up with the center front of the garment, color code the quarter marks. Use multi-colored glass bead pins and choose 2 red ones to mark the center fronts. The other quarter marks can be any color other than red. When pinning the ribbing and shirt together, match the 2 red glass-bead pins and the other quarter marks.

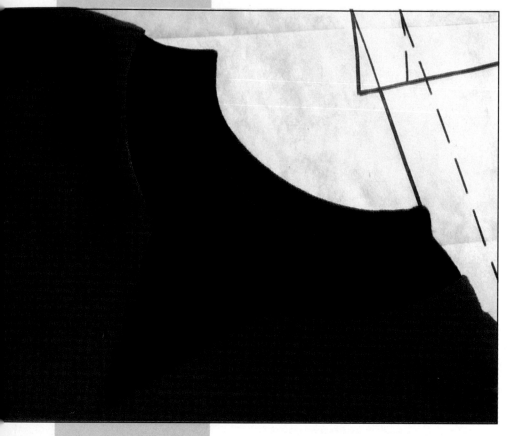

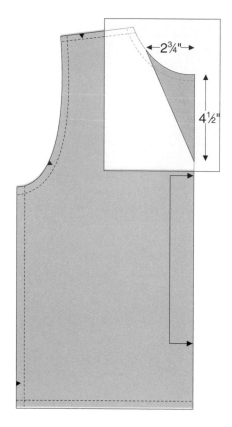

Sweatshirt V-Accent
20 Minutes

Sweatshirts endure as a sportswear mainstay. Update this comfortable classic with a simple-to-sew V-shaped accent.

1. To make the sweatshirt V-accent pattern (The size of the V can be varied as desired):

• Fold the sweatshirt pattern in half and mark the center front.

• Cover the top center front area with tissue or waxed paper.

• On the paper, mark 4½" down the center front line from the neckline.

• Mark 2¾" from the center front line to a point on the original pattern neckline.

• Connect the 2 marked points, forming a V-shape. Trace the marked area to make a pattern. Add a ¼" seam allowance on the long side of the V pattern.

2. To cut out fabrics for the V:

• Cut 1 insert of interlock or ribbing. Mark the center front with a V-clip. Also V-clip the center front of the sweatshirt.

• Cut a second insert from fusible-knit interfacing, such as Stacy's Easy Knit.

3. To sew the insert:

• Align the right side of the insert with the fusible (resin) side of the interfacing.

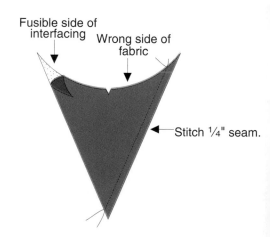

• Serge or sew 1 side of the V, using a ¼" seam.

• At the point, wrap the seam allowance toward the center of the V. (Wrapping makes it much easier to turn a smooth, uniform corner.)

• Stitch the second straight side of the V, using a ¼" seam.

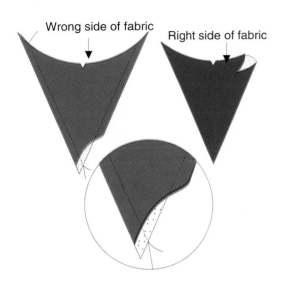

Wrong side of fabric   Right side of fabric

• Trim the seam allowances at the point to reduce bulk.

• Turn the V accent right side out. Use a Bamboo Pointer and Creaser to obtain sharp corners. Finger-press the edges.

4. Place the fusible side of the V on the right side of the sweatshirt, matching center-front V-clips.

5. Cover the V with an Appliqué Pressing Sheet and fuse the V to the sweatshirt.

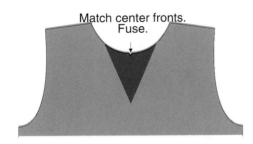

Match center fronts.
Fuse.

6. Edgestitch ⅛" to ¼" from the sides of the V accent.

Edgestitch. →

7. Continue following your pattern instructions to complete the shirt.

Split Collar
10 Minutes

If you follow trendy fashions, you know that this neckline variation is all the rage. Made from ribbing or interlock, the collar can be worn up for a sophisticated look or turned down for a more casual look.

To make the split collar:

1. To determine the collar size:

• Length: Overlap the pattern front and back pieces at the shoulder seams. Determine the neckline circumference by measuring along the stitching line. An easy way to accurately determine the collar length measurement is to place the tape measure on its edge along the stitching line. The tape will follow the curve more easily in this position. (If patterns are cut on the fold, remember to double the neckline circumference measurement.) To the neckline circumference, add 2 seam allowances (usually ½" total).

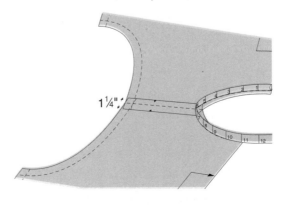

1¼"

Note from Nancy

To press the V accent flat, sandwich the finished piece between 2 layers of an Appliqué Pressing Sheet and press. After the fabric cools, the fusible side of the V can be easily peeled off the non-stick Teflon surface of the pressing sheet.

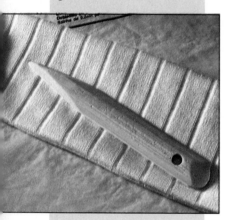

• Width: For adults, cut the collar 10" wide. For children, cut the collar 6" wide.

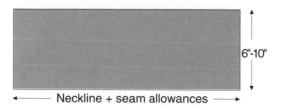

Neckline + seam allowances

2. For the adult sizes, mark 2½" from the cut edges. For children's sizes, mark 1½" from the cut edges.

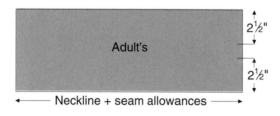

Adult's

Neckline + seam allowances

Child's

3. To sew the center back collar seam:
• Fold the collar in half widthwise, with right sides together. Stitch from the cut edge to the mark. Lock the stitching; clip the threads. Repeat from the other cut edge to the other mark.

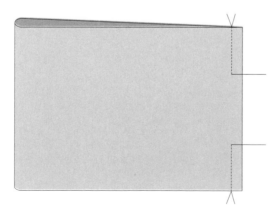

• Refold the ribbing so that the marked ends of the first stitchings meet. Stitch from 1 fold to the center; lock the stitches. Repeat from the other fold. It's important that these stitchings come as close to the center as possible without stitching into the center. Otherwise you'll end up with a hole in the center of the split collar.

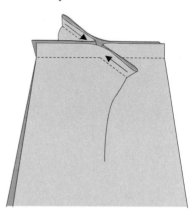

• Angle-cut the corners to remove excess bulk. Turn the collar right side out and fold in half with raw edges together. Finger-press.

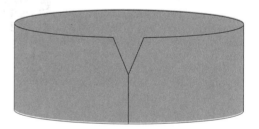

4. Quarter-mark the collar and the neckline edge. Serge or straightstitch the collar to the neckline, positioning the split at the center front.

Double Ribbing
10 Minutes

Double your wardrobe versatility with this double ribbing. Experiment with different color combinations and widths of ribbing.

To prepare the ribbing:

1. If your shirt pattern contains a pattern piece for the ribbing, simply add 1" to the length for 1 piece of ribbing. (The extra inch is necessary because the neckline becomes tighter with 2 thicknesses of ribbing; the extra length adds the necessary "give.")

2. Cut a second piece of ribbing, either wider or narrower than the first, and the same length as the first ribbing piece.

• To determine the second ribbing width: Double the finished width plus ½"—for 2 (¼") seam allowances. For example, a ribbing piece measuring 6½" wide will make a 3"-wide finished trim.

3. To sew the ribbing:

• For 1 ribbing piece, straightstitch each end seam, with right sides together. Finger-press the seams open. Repeat with the other ribbing piece.

• Turn each ribbing piece right side out and place the long cut edges together.

• Zigzag or serge the 2 ribbings together at the cut edges, using a narrow serge or zigzag stitch.

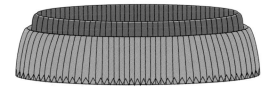

• With pins, quarter-mark the ribbing and the neckline of the garment.

• Align the pins and sew or serge the ribbing to the garment, using a zigzag or serged stitch wide enough to cover the previous stitching.

Note from Nancy

*Here is how to figure the ribbing size if your pattern doesn't include a pattern piece for it. Ribbing is generally applied at a 2:3 ratio. So cut the ribbing ⅔ the length of the neckline measurement. For example, if the neckline measures 18":
⅔ x 18 = 12" + ½"= 12½" collar length. For children, the ratio is often 3:4. Because a child's head is larger in proportion to the rest of his body, you'll need to cut the ribbing ¾ the length of the neckline.*

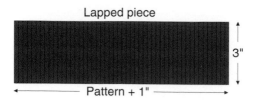

Lapped piece

3"

Pattern + 1"

2. Fold the lapped piece in half lengthwise, with wrong sides together. Mark 1" from each end along the cut edge. Trim the ends at an angle, beginning at the 1" mark and tapering to the fold.

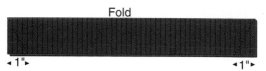

Fold

◄1"► ◄1"►

3. Overlap the ends 1", aligning the cut edges at the bottom. Straightstitch, zigzag, or serge the cut edges together, rounding off the corners. Quarter-mark the lapped piece, placing the first pin at the center of the overlap.

4. Straightstitch or serge the ¼" center back seam of the crew-neckline piece. Fold the ribbing in half lengthwise, with wrong sides together; straightstitch, zigzag, or serge the cut edges together. Quarter-mark the crew neckline piece, placing the first pin at the seam.

5. Align the quarter marks and the cut edges of the ribbed pieces, with the lapped piece on top. Place the crew neckline seam directly opposite the lapped piece. Machine-baste the cut edges together.

Baste cut edges together, rounding corners.

6. Quarter-mark the garment neckline. With right sides together, align the overlapped ribbing with the neckline edge. Place the crew neckline seam at the center back and the center of the lapped piece at the center front. Straightstitch or serge the neckline seam through all layers.

Ribbed Baseball Neckline

—20 Minutes—

Your whole family will want shirts featuring this lapped ribbed neckline. Try using 2 different colors of ribbing. Before cutting out the ribbing, experiment to determine which color you want to be dominant.

To make the baseball neckline:

1. Cut 2 ribbing pieces, using the pattern to determine the length.

• For the crew neckline piece, cut the ribbing 4" wide.

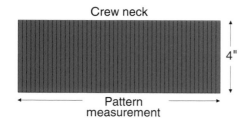

Crew neck

4"

Pattern
measurement

• For the lapped piece, cut a piece of ribbing 3" wide and 1" longer than the crew neckline piece.

Johnny Collar
—30 Minutes—

You'll like the Johnny collar's convertibility. It can be worn turned down (over the ribbing), standing up, or pinned to 1 side. In this technique, the collar is added after the ribbing has been applied. If you can't find just the right purchased collar, here's how to make your own.

To make the Johnny collar:

1. To determine the collar size:

• Measure around the seam line where the ribbing has been attached.

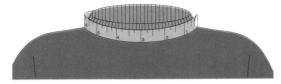

• The collar length is ¾ the length of the garment neckline measurement plus ½"—for 2 (¼") seam allowances. If the neckline measurement is 18", the collar length is 14".

• An average finished collar width is 4". Double this finished width and add ½"—for 2 (¼") seam allowances. The ribbing size in this example would be 8½" x 14".

2. Cut the collar from the ribbing.

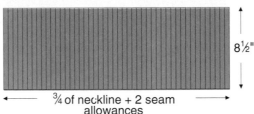

¾ of neckline + 2 seam allowances

8½"

3. Fold the collar in half lengthwise, with right sides together; straightstitch each end using the ¼" seams.

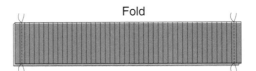

Fold

4. Turn the collar right side out. Finger-press if necessary, but do not press with an iron.

5. Overlap the collar center front edges by ½". Machine-baste or zigzag to secure the overlap.

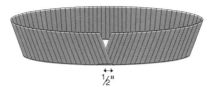

½"

6. Quarter-mark the collar and neckline edges.

7. Match the center front and back of garment and collar; pin.

8. Machine-stitch the collar to the neckline, using the original ribbing seam line as a guide for stitching.

Note from Nancy

Use your tape measure as a calculator! To determine ¾ of 18", fold the end of the tape measure to the 18" mark. Then fold a second time. The measurement on the fold is 13½"—¾ of 18". Add ½" (¼" on each side) for seam allowances.

83

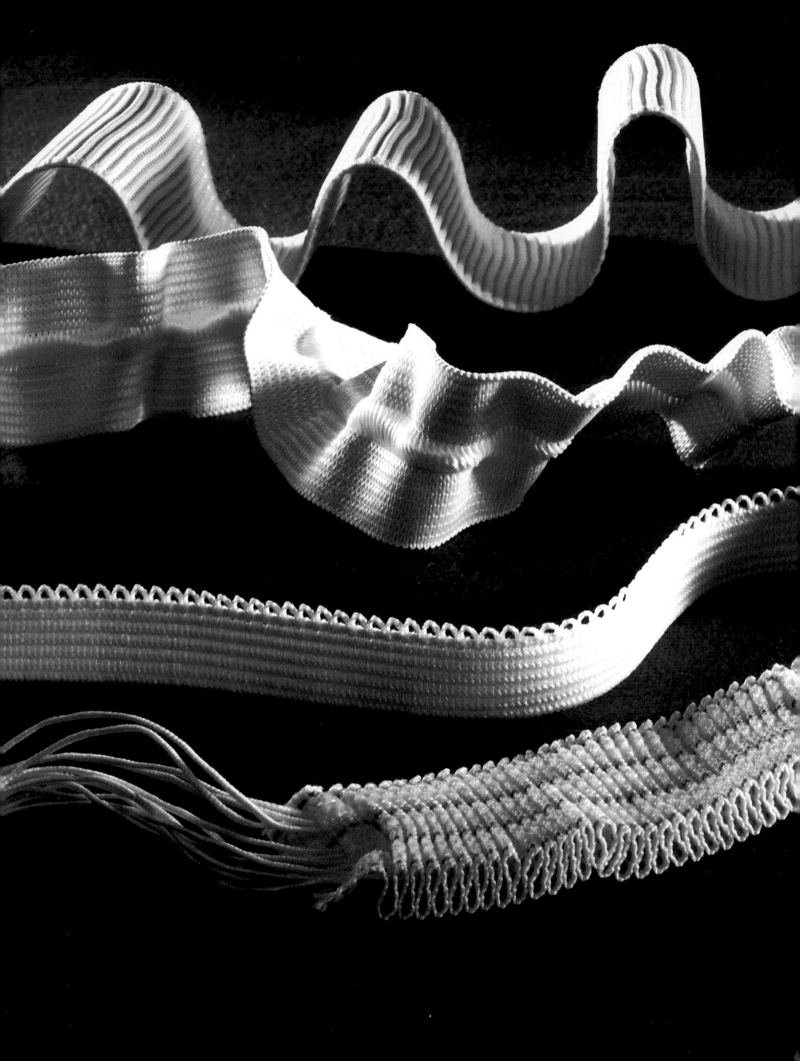

Elastics
FAST AND FUN TO SEW

Elastic is the perfect choice to finish active and casual wear for the entire family. Use it in waistbands for pants, skirts, or shorts, as well as on cuffs or sleeves. With all the different types of elastic available to home sewers, its stitching possibilities are almost endless.

Elastic
I.D.

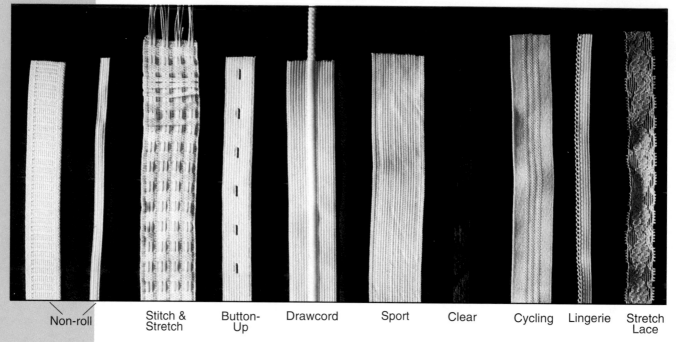

Non-roll | Stitch & Stretch | Button-Up | Drawcord | Sport | Clear | Cycling | Lingerie | Stretch Lace

Basic Elastics

Non-roll elastics are made by knitting elastic threads together. Because they retain their shape when stretched, non-roll elastics are more suitable for most applications than braided elastics. Non-roll elastics are generally ¼" to 2" wide and can be used in casings, or sewn or serged directly to the fabric.

Braided elastic generally costs less than non-roll elastic, but it narrows when it is stretched. Because it changes shape, you should use this elastic only in a casing.

Specialty Elastics

Stitch & Stretch, a woven polyester band with rows of spandex elastic cording, is 1 of the newest specialty elastics. It is stitched flat to the fabric along the woven-in blue lines (no need to stretch the elastic as you sew), and then the spandex cords are pulled to gather the fabric to the correct size. It is available in 1", 1½", and 2¼" widths.

Button-Up Elastic is a ¾"-wide polyester-and-rubber elastic with woven buttonhole sections in the center of the band. The buttonhole openings are spaced 1" apart. A button is sewn inside the casing for easy waistline adjustments.

Drawcord Elastic has a drawcord knitted into the 1¼"-wide band that will extend to twice its length, allowing ample cord for tying inside or outside the waistband.

Sport Elastic, an elastic used in ready-to-wear sportswear, can be stitched directly to the fabric. The 4 unbraided rows provide guides for stitching.

Clear Elastic is a transparent strip of durable 100% polyurethane that stretches to 3 times its original length. It is lightweight and resists deterioration by swimming pool chlorine, yet is durable enough to be stitched through (or even nicked by serger blades) without losing its elasticity.

Cycling Elastic is ideal for use with Lycra. Three rows of exposed spandex threads grip the skin, keeping garments from "riding up."

Lingerie Elastic is a soft elastic with a decorative picot edge, available in ¼" and ½" widths. Another soft elastic, often used on expensive ready-made lingerie, is **Stretch Lace**.

Non-roll and Braided Elastic *Techniques*

Updated Elastic Casing

Here's the most professional elastic application for casual wear. Use ¾" or 1" non-roll elastic for the best results. The key to this technique is using a zipper foot.

1. Sew or serge the side seams of the garment.

2. Fold and press a 1½" casing. (This is the common width allowed for casings on patterns.) Zigzag or serge the raw edge.

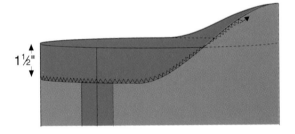

3. Edgestitch ⅛" from the fold.

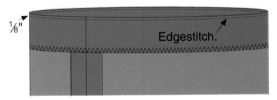

Edgestitch.

4. Cut the elastic 2" shorter than the waistline measurement.

5. Butt the elastic ends together. Place a scrap of tightly woven fabric under the elastic ends. Zigzag the elastic ends to the fabric. Trim away the excess fabric.

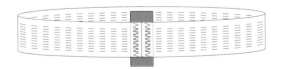

6. Place the elastic inside the casing, stretching the elastic to fit and periodically pinning it in place.

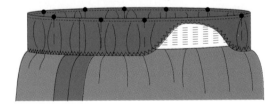

7. Use a zipper foot with the needle positioned at the right side of the foot. With the edge of the foot next to the elastic, sew, smoothing the fabric so that it lies flat in front of the foot. Allow the fabric to gather behind the foot. The elastic will be tightly sandwiched between the 2 rows of straight-stitching, producing a professional look.

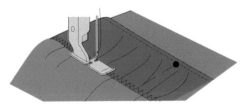

Note from Nancy

I used to join elastic in a circle by overlapping the ends of the elastic ½" and zigzagging them together. However, the scrap of fabric works much better. The double layer of elastic created bulk at the seam, and the waistband would not lie flat.

3. Stitch the center seams and 1 side seam, leaving the remaining side seam unstitched.

4. Using a ⅝" seam on your conventional machine, stitch the remaining side seam from the lower edge of the garment to the casing fold line. Do not serge. (The wider, pressed-open seam allowance of the conventional stitch will make it easier to insert the elastic.)

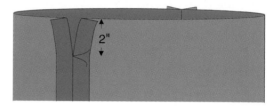

5. From the casing fold line, leave a 1¾" opening in the seam by advancing the fabric through the sewing machine. Stitch the final ¼" of the seam to close the ends of the casing.

6. Trim the seam allowances within the casing area to ⅜".

7. Fuse all the seam allowances within the casing to the garment with a narrow strip of fusible web, such as Stitch Witchery or Wonder-Under. This will prevent the seam allowances from blocking the elastic when it's being inserted in the casing. In this example, the strips of fusible web would be 4" long (double the casing width).

Fusible web

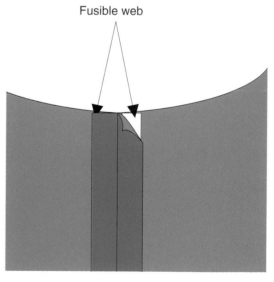

Three-Row Elastic Casing
20 Minutes

Add interest to a waistline by using multiple rows of elastic. This is a functional, fashionable waistline treatment that is slightly wider than the casing found on most patterns.

To make the casing:

1. Cut 3 strips of ⅜"-wide elastic, each 2" shorter than the waistline measurement.

2. Check the casing width allowed on the pattern and extend the pattern as necessary to provide 2" for the casing. Cut out the garment.

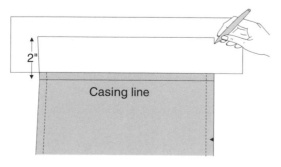

2"

Casing line

8. Fold the fabric to the wrong side of the garment along the casing fold line; press. Zigzag or serge the raw edge.

9. Start ½" from the casing fold and straightstitch 3 rows, ½" apart.

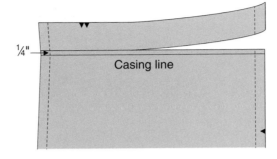

½"
½"
½"

10. Insert 1 strip of elastic through each row of the casing with a bodkin, safety pin, or elastic glide. (Before inserting the elastic, pin 1 end to the fabric to keep it from being pulled into the casing.)

11. Butt the elastic ends together. Place a scrap of tightly woven fabric under the elastic. Zigzag the elastic ends to the fabric. Trim away the excess fabric.

12. Stretch the waistline to evenly distribute the fabric.

13. Stitch in-the-ditch (sew from the right side into the seam line) along each side seam of the casing. This stitching will keep the elastic evenly distributed and prevent it from twisting.

Action Wear Waistband

Examine a piece of ready-made action wear and you'll find this durable covered waistband. Suited to both knit and woven fabrics, this waistband is fashionable and easy to produce. Just use some non-roll elastic and a little sewing know-how to modify the waistband pattern in any pair of pants or shorts.

1. Mark a new cutting line on the pattern, ¼" above the casing fold line. (You must remove the excess casing because the elastic will be inserted inside a separate waistband.)

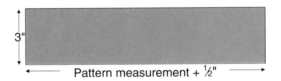

¼"

Casing line

2. Cut a separate waistband 3" wide and as long as the garment waistline measurement plus ½". With right sides together, sew the ends of the waistband together, forming a circle.

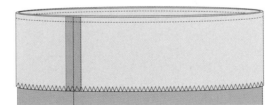

3"

Pattern measurement + ½"

3. With right sides together, stitch the waistband to the top of the assembled garment, using a ¼" seam.

Timesaving Notions

A bodkin is my favorite notion for inserting elastic into a casing. Special teeth grip the elastic so that it doesn't get lost inside the casing.

An Elastic Glide has 1 small rounded end and a wider, slotted end into which the elastic is threaded. The long glide prevents the elastic from twisting in the casing during insertion. To accommodate different sizes of elastic, glides come in widths of ¼", ½", and ¾".

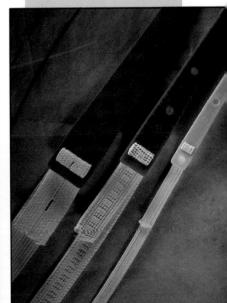

Note from Nancy

To prevent the waistband from shifting during the final stitching, baste through the elastic and waistband at each quarter mark before stitching. (This helps keep the gathers in the band perfectly vertical.) Lengthen the stitch and leave long thread tails at each end of the basting so that they can be easily removed later.

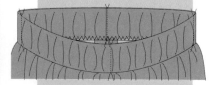

Timesaving Notions

Available in both ⅝" and 1¼" widths, Seams Great is a bias-cut 100% nylon tricot binding traditionally used to clean-finish seam allowances. Since it's soft and extremely lightweight, it adds virtually no bulk—something that's really important in a casing. Use the 1¼" width with ½" or ⅝" elastic; use the ⅝" width with very narrow elastics.

4. Cut a length of 1"-wide non-roll elastic, 2" shorter than the waistline measurement. Butt the elastic ends together. Place a scrap of tightly woven fabric under the elastic and zigzag the elastic ends to the fabric. Trim away the excess fabric.

5. Quarter-mark the elastic and the waistband. With the waistband still against the garment, pin the elastic to the waistband seam allowance, matching the quarter marks, aligning the lower edge of the elastic with the seam line joining the garment and waistband, and allowing the elastic to extend above the garment. Baste in place.

6. Zigzag the elastic to the ¼" seam allowance, stretching the elastic as necessary to match the quarter marks.

7. Wrap the waistband over the elastic to the wrong side of the garment. Pin.

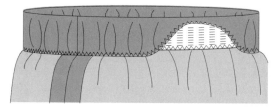

8. Working from the right side of the garment and stretching the elastic as you stitch, straightstitch the lower edge of the waistband ⅛" above the waistline seam. Don't stitch through the elastic. Straightstitch the upper edge of the waistband in the same manner.

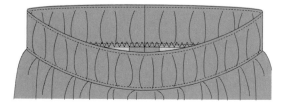

9. Remove the basting stitches.

Seams Great Elastic Casing
—— *10 Minutes* ——

This elastic insertion technique uses traditional non-roll or braided elastic—but in a very lightweight casing. Often, when a pattern includes an elastic casing at the waistline, the guide sheet will suggest using strips of bias-cut fabric or bias tape to form the casing. This extra layer of bias fabric may result in a bulky, uncomfortable waistline. Here's a quick, lightweight way to achieve the same elasticized waistline.

1. Mark the placement line for the elastic on the wrong side of the garment, using a washable marking pen, marking pencil, or chalk.

2. Fold under ¼" on 1 end of a matching or coordinating color of Seams Great. Align the fold at 1 of the garment's side seams.

3. Stitch 1 edge of the Seams Great around the waistline, ⅛" to ¼" from the edge. When you come to the end of the Seams Great, turn under ¼" and butt it against the other turned-under end of the casing.

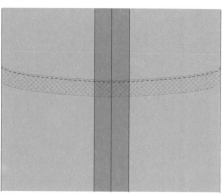

4. Tuck the elastic underneath the Seams Great casing. (Remember, the elastic must be narrower than the casing.) Secure 1 end of the elastic to the casing by bar tacking with 2 or 3 stitches. Bar-tack in-the-ditch of the side seam, if possible, to conceal the stitching.

5. To stitch the remaining edge of the casing:

• Remove the general-purpose presser foot and replace it with a zipper foot. Adjust the needle position so that the needle is as close as possible to the right edge of the zipper foot.

• Position the zipper foot next to the elastic and stitch along the other edge of the Seams Great, encasing the elastic. Do not stitch through the elastic.

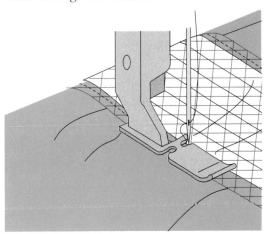

6. Try on the garment and pull the elastic to fit. Bar-tack to secure the elastic and close the opening. Cut away the excess elastic.

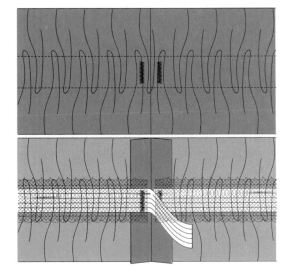

Note from Nancy

If your sewing machine has a free arm, here's an ideal place to use it. Since the waistline is a circle, the project slips easily over the free arm, making it easier to stitch the casing.

Note from Nancy

It's easier to insert the elastic and stitch the remaining casing edge before the elastic is cut to size. Mark the finished length on the elastic to serve as a guide before inserting it, but do not cut it until the casing is completely stitched.

Quick Elastic Casing for Sleeves

For a simple elastic treatment on cuffs and sleeves for children's wear, zigzag over a length of very narrow elastic to create a casing. Create this casing before sewing the underarm seam of the sleeve.

To create the quick casing:

1. Cut a length of ⅛"- or ¼"-wide elastic to a comfortable measurement for the child's wrist or arm. (Be sure to add 1¼" to the measured length for seam allowances.)

2. Place the elastic on the wrong side of the sleeve along the gathering line. Pin at each cut edge.

3. Bar-tack the elastic to the seam allowance at 1 end.

4. Set the sewing machine at a medium stitch length and a zigzag stitch wider than the elastic.

5. Stretch the elastic across the sleeve, holding the fabric taut both in front and behind the presser foot. Zigzag *over* the elastic, making sure not to catch the elastic in the stitching.

6. Bar-tack the other end of the elastic to the fabric.

7. Sew the sleeve seam. It's that fast and simple!

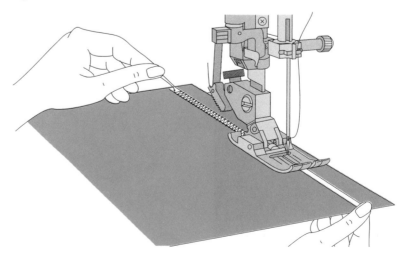

SPECIALTY Elastics

Stitch & Stretch

Stitch & Stretch is 1 of the newest elastics. It is stitched to the flat garment and then stretched. This woven polyester band has rows of spandex elastic threaded through it. Non-elastic blue lines running the length of the band provide convenient stitching guides.

To apply the elastic:

1. Stitch the center seams and 1 of the garment's side seams. (Remember: This elastic is stitched to the flat fabric.)

2. Press the casing to the wrong side of the garment. Trim the casing to ½".

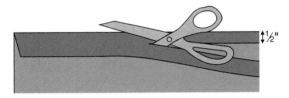

3. Cut the Stitch & Stretch elastic the *same length* as the unfinished waistline. (Stitch & Stretch is the exception to the rule of cutting elastic smaller than the finished waistline.)

4. To position the elastic:

• Fold under ½" on 1 end of the Stitch & Stretch. Place the elastic on the wrong side of the garment, with the upper edge of the elastic ⅛" from the fold at the top of the waistband.

• Zigzag the folded end of the elastic to the garment to secure the elastic cords.

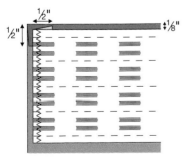

• On the opposite end of the Stitch & Stretch, fold under only the woven fabric, not the elastic cords. (The cords must be free so that they can be pulled to gather the

waistband to its finished size.) Pin the Stitch & Stretch in place.

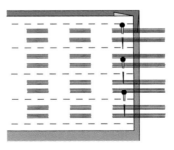

5. Sew the Stitch & Stretch to the garment along each of the blue stitching lines.

6. Pull the elastic cords until the waistband is the desired finished size. Evenly distribute the gathers. Then secure the cords at the end of the Stitch & Stretch by zigzagging ⅜" to ½" from the cut edge. For greater security, add a second line of zigzag stitching ¼" from the edge. Trim away the excess cords.

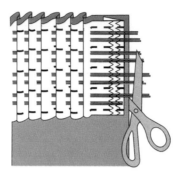

7. Stitch the remaining side seam.

Stitch & Stretch: An Enclosed Technique

The basic exposed Stitch & Stretch application is suited to most garments. But there may be times when you prefer to enclose the elastic, rather than exposing it.

Before cutting out the garment, check the pattern to be sure that the casing on the pattern is slightly wider than the elastic. This is especially important when you are using the 2¼"-wide Stitch & Stretch.

1. Stitch the center seams and 1 of the garment's side seams.

2. Press the casing to the wrong side to establish the fold line. *Do not* trim away any of the casing; the casing must be wide enough to cover the elastic.

3. To apply the Stitch & Stretch to the garment:

• Cut the Stitch & Stretch the same length as the casing.

• Position the elastic on the wrong side of the garment, with the edge of the elastic along the casing fold line. (The elastic should be positioned on the garment section, not on the casing.)

• Stitch the elastic to the garment, using Steps 4-6 in the basic Stitch & Stretch directions.

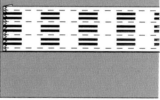

4. Fold the casing to cover the elastic. Pin the casing in place from the right side of the garment.

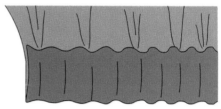

5. Stitch the casing closed from the right side of the garment, sewing along the upper row of the original stitching. Stretch the fabric to fit as you stitch. The elastic will be completely encased.

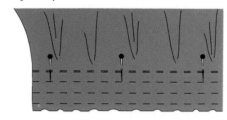

6. Stitch the remaining side seam of the garment.

Button-Up Elastic— It's Adjustable

A waistline with breathing room? You can create it with this elastic with buttonholes! The sewing is simple; just add a button to the inside of the casing. Use it in clothing for growing children, for moms-to-be, or for anyone with a changing waistline.

1. Cut the elastic longer than needed for the waistline, especially when making maternity wear.

2. Stitch the garment's center seams and 1 side seam, leaving the remaining side seam open to insert the elastic.

• On the final side seam, use your conventional machine and a ⅝" seam to stitch from the lower edge to the casing fold line. At the fold line, backstitch or stitch in place to reinforce the seam.

• From the casing fold line, leave a 1" opening in the seam by advancing the fabric through the sewing machine. Stitch the final ¼" of the seam to close the ends of the casing.

3. Trim the seam allowance to ⅜" within the casing area. Fuse this section of the seam to the garment with narrow strips of fusible web.

4. Fold the casing to the wrong side of the garment along the fold line. Press.

5. Unfold the casing. Mark the button placement on the inside of the casing, next to the casing opening. Stitching through the casing layer only, attach a button that will fit through the buttonhole openings in the elastic.

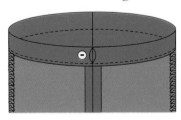

6. Refold the casing to the wrong side of the garment. Stitch the casing, sewing completely around the lower edge.

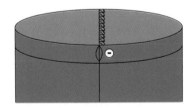

7. Secure 1 end of the elastic to the seam opening by stitching in-the-ditch. Insert the elastic through the casing, using a bodkin or elastic glide.

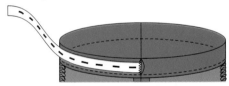

8. Pull the elastic to the desired size. Secure the free end of the elastic to the garment by buttoning it over the button.

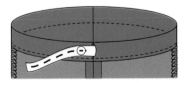

9. Conceal the remaining end of the elastic by tucking it into the unstitched opening. When more room (or less) is needed, just rebutton!

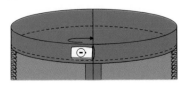

Note from Nancy

With Button-Up elastic, the casing is left open at 1 of the seams. I prefer to set this opening at 1 of the side seams to prevent the button from pressing against the small of the back. Also, be sure to stitch this final seam with your conventional machine using a standard ⅝" seam, rather than with a serger. The wider, pressed-open seam allowance makes it easier to insert the elastic.

Note from Nancy

It's essential to keep the ends of the drawcord out of the way, so that they aren't caught in the zigzag stitching. Otherwise, you will not be able to pull the drawcord through the elastic.

Timesaving Notions

To provide additional support when stitching these buttonholes, place a piece of Stitch-N-Tear stabilizer under the fabric before making the buttonholes. Remove the stabilizer after the buttonhole is completed. The stabilizer prevents the buttonholes from sinking into the fabric.

Drawcord Elastic
—20 Minutes—

Make your next pair of jogging pants or shorts with Drawcord Elastic, a 1¼"-wide elastic with a drawcord knitted into the middle. This specialty elastic designed for active wear is extremely flexible; the drawcord can be tightened *after* the elastic has been applied. This application takes just a few extra minutes to complete because you must make 2 small buttonholes to accommodate the drawcord.

1. Sew the side garment seams.

2. Cut the elastic 2" shorter than the waist measurement.

3. At each end of the elastic, cut about ½" of the threads that cover the drawcord.

4. Overlap the ends of the elastic by ¼", keeping the cords free. Zigzag the ends of the elastic together several times.

5. To determine the placement of the buttonholes for the drawcord:

• For a drawcord hidden on the inside of the garment, stitch 1 vertical ½" buttonhole on each side of the center front seam, with the top of the buttonholes ½" from the top edge of the waistband. When the casing is folded to the inside, these buttonholes will be on the inside of the garment.

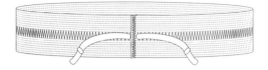

• For an exposed drawcord (as shown in photo), begin stitching the top of the buttonholes 1½" from the top edge of the waistband. These buttonholes will remain on the outside of the garment when the casing is folded to the inside.

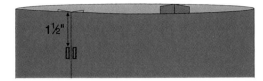

• Cut the buttonholes open.

6. Quarter-mark both the elastic and the garment waistband; pin the elastic to the garment at each mark. If the drawcord will be hidden on the inside of the garment, place the *right* side of the elastic against the wrong side of the garment. If the drawcord will be exposed, place the *wrong* side of the elastic to the wrong side of the garment.

7. Serge or zigzag the elastic to the top edge of the waistband, stretching the elastic as you sew.

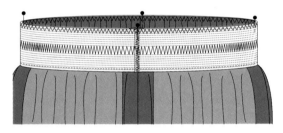

8. Fold the elastic and waistband to the wrong side of the garment. (Check to be sure the waistband fabric is securely wrapped around the elastic.)

9. Baste through the elastic and the garment at each quarter mark to hold the casing and elastic in position for the final stitching.

10. Thread the drawcords through the buttonholes.

11. Straightstitch or zigzag around the entire waistband along the lower edge of the casing, stretching the elastic to fit. Remove the basting stitches.

12. Pull up the cords to gather the waistband and knot each end. Tie cords into a bow. Voila! A ready-made touch!

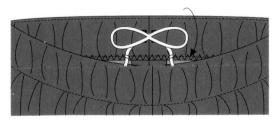

Sew-Through Sport Elastic
—— *20 Minutes* ——

In 20 minutes or less, you can duplicate the look of topstitched elastic used on ready-to-wear garments by using Sew-Through Sport Elastic. This 1¼"- or 1½"-wide elastic has 4 unbraided rows that serve as guidelines when stitching the elastic to the garment. Most other elastics will stretch out of shape when topstitched to the waistline, because the sewing machine needle cuts the rubberized, stretchable threads. In Sew-Through Sport Elastic, the rubberized threads are left out of the unbraided rows, preventing the pesky problem with stitching.

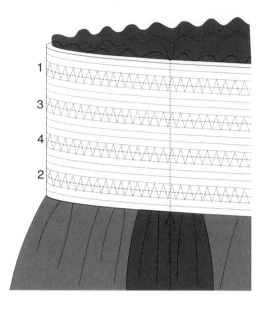

1. Stitch the side seams of the garment to form the waistband. Press the casing to the wrong side, forming a fold line, and trim the waistband casing to ½".

2. Fuse the ½" casing to the garment fabric with a narrow strip of fusible web. (This stabilizes the waistband and prevents it from stretching out of shape.)

Fusible web

3. Cut the elastic 3" to 5" shorter than your waistline measurement. (To decide whether you should cut the elastic 3" or 5", take a few seconds to pin the elastic into a circle at the 3" and 5" measurements. Check to see which measurement fits most comfortably over your hipline.)

4. Butt the elastic ends together. Place a scrap of tightly woven fabric under the elastic ends. Zigzag the elastic ends to the fabric. Trim away the excess fabric.

5. Quarter-mark the elastic and the waistband. Pin the elastic to the waistband, matching pins; place the seam in the elastic at the center back of the garment. Place the top edge of the elastic ¼" to ⅜" from the casing fold.

6. Stitch in-the-ditch at all seams to secure the elastic. If the garment seams don't line up with the quarter marks, machine-baste the elastic to the garment at the quarter marks and remove the basting stitches later.

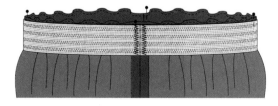

7. Stitch the elastic from the wrong side along the unbraided rows, stretching the elastic to fit the waistband. For best results, stitch the rows in this sequence: top row, bottom row, and then the 2 middle rows.

Clear Elastic

Clear Elastic, a 100% polyurethane elastic that is new on the market, is designed specifically to be used in aerobic wear and swimwear. It stretches to 3 times its original length and has 3 unique features. First, it's 100% recoverable! Once stretched, it will return to its original length and width. Second, it is not affected by chlorine, making Clear Elastic perfect for swimwear. And third, this elastic will not fray or ravel if nicked by the serger blade—a remarkable feature!

Clear Elastic is available in a variety of widths, including ¼", ⅜", ½", and ¾".

Swimwear Elastic Guidelines

Refer to your pattern directions, or use these general guidelines for measuring the elastic.

• Leg opening: For adult sizes, cut the elastic 2" shorter than the pattern measurement for the leg opening. For children's sizes, cut the elastic 1" shorter than the leg opening.

• Waistline: Cut the elastic 4" to 6" shorter than a comfortable waistline measurement.

• Armhole: Cut the elastic the same size as the armhole pattern measurement.

• Neckline: Cut the elastic the same size as the neckline pattern measurement.

Leg Opening Sewing Guidelines

1. To join the front and back of the swimsuit, stitch the crotch seam.

2. Without stretching the elastic, pin it to the wrong side of the leg front, from the front edge to the crotch seam.

3. Divide the remaining elastic in half and mark with a pin. Divide the back leg opening in half and mark with a pin. Pin the elastic to the leg opening, matching the pins.

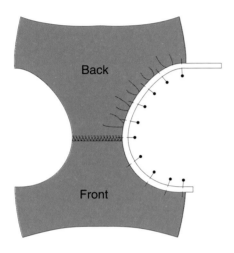

4. Sew or serge the elastic to the leg opening, stretching the elastic as needed to meet the fabric. Repeat for the other leg opening.

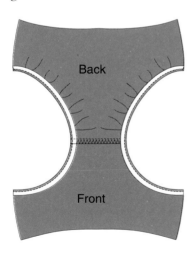

5. Cut off any excess elastic.

6. Serge or sew the side seams.

7. Turn the elastic to the wrong side and topstitch, preferably using a double needle.

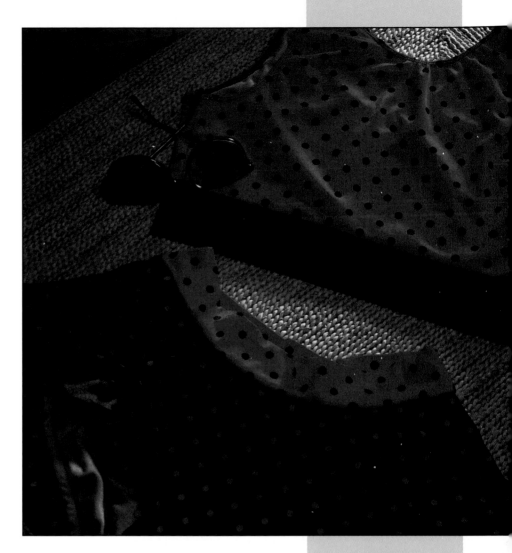

(The double-needle topstitching adds stretch to the stitching and gives the swimsuit a ready-to-wear sportswear look.)

Note from Nancy

Instead of cutting the elastic before sewing it to the swimsuit, mark the needed size directly on the length of elastic with a ballpoint pen. (Felt-tip or washable markers will not leave a lasting mark on the smooth plastic surface.) After stitching the elastic to the garment opening, cut the elastic at the ink mark. The extra length of elastic gives you something to grasp while stretching the elastic to fit the opening.

Super-Quick Gathering with Clear Elastic

Clear Elastic isn't just for swimwear. Since its stretch and retention aren't damaged by stitching through it, try using ⅜" or ½" Clear Elastic to gather both knit and woven fabrics. The elastic is practically invisible and adds almost no bulk to the gathers.

Measure your waist (or where the elastic is to be used) to determine the finished length of the garment opening to be gathered. Cut a length of Clear Elastic this finished length plus 1¼" for seam allowances. Quarter-mark the elastic and the garment.

With the elastic against the wrong side of the fabric, match the quarter marks; pin. At each end of the fabric, align the end of the Clear Elastic with the cut edge of the fabric; pin the elastic ⅝" from each end, leaving a loose extension of elastic within the seam allowance. (This extension will provide a "tail" for you to grasp, helping to stretch the elastic while stitching it in place.)

Place the fabric under the presser foot. With your machine set at its widest zigzag, stretch the elastic to fit the fabric and stitch, beginning and ending ⅝" from the edge.

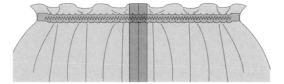

Cycling Elastic

As the name implies, Cycling Elastic is perfect for making cycling pants or shorts. This elastic is 1" wide with exposed rows of rubber that "grip" the skin, giving the needed tight fit.

1. Set your machine for a zigzag stitch and use a Stretch, Yellow Band, or ballpoint needle.

2. Determine the length of elastic needed. Cut the elastic for the waistline 2" shorter than your comfortable waistline measurement. For the leg opening, cut the elastic the length of the pattern measurement.

3. Butt the ends of the elastic together. Place a scrap of tightly woven fabric under the elastic ends. Zigzag the elastic to the fabric. Trim away the excess fabric.

4. Sew the side seams, inseams, and crotch seam of the pants.

5. On the right side of the fabric at the waistband and the leg openings, mark the ⅝" seam allowance with a washable marking pen.

6. Align 1 edge of the elastic with the ⅝" seam marking on the right side of the garment. Pin the elastic to the fabric, aligning the seam in the elastic with the center back seam of the garment.

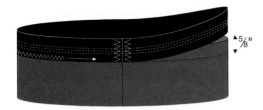

7. Zigzag the edge of the elastic to the garment along the marked seam line, using a medium stitch width and length.

8. Trim away the excess seam allowance. Fold the elastic to the wrong side of the garment. Zigzag the elastic to the garment along the remaining edge.

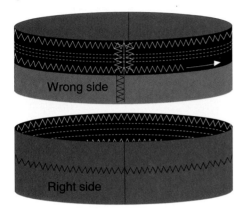

Wrong side

Right side

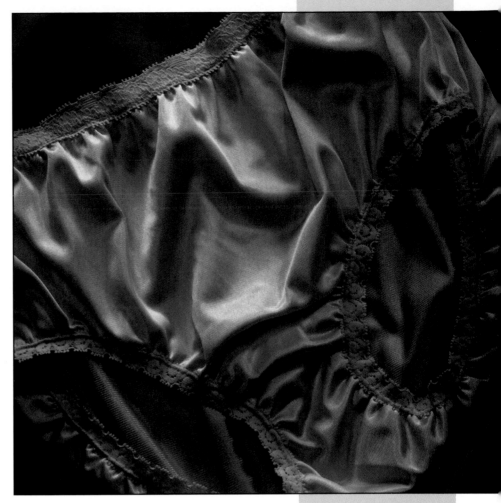

Stretch Lingerie Lace

There are many ways of applying elastic to lingerie. The preferred method involves Stretch Lace—decorative, yet soft next to the skin. It comes in a variety of widths: a wide lace for the waist and narrower widths for the legs. Stretch Lace also has the necessary amount of stretch for briefs, panties, or slips, and adds a feminine touch.

1. Determine the length of elastic needed. Cut the elastic for the waistline 2" shorter than your comfortable waistline measurement, plus ½" for seam allowances. For the leg openings, cut each length of elastic 2" shorter than the pattern measurement, plus ½" for seam allowances.

2. Use a good quality, 100% polyester thread and a Stretch, Yellow Band, or ballpoint needle. Stitch all except 1 side seam of the garment.

3. Quarter-mark the leg openings, waistband, and all lengths of elastic.

4. Place the *wrong* side of the elastic on the *right* side of the garment, aligning the top edge of the elastic with the cut edge of the fabric.

5. Pin the elastic to the garment, matching the quarter marks.

6. Zigzag the lower edge of the elastic in place, using a medium stitch width and length. Stretch the elastic to match the fabric.

7. Trim away the excess seam allowance.

Timesaving Notions

Appliqué scissors, the 6" scissors with the duck-bill blade, can be used for more than appliqué work. When you are trimming seam allowances, place the duck-bill under the fabric to be trimmed; the larger blade allows you to trim closely without cutting the elastic.

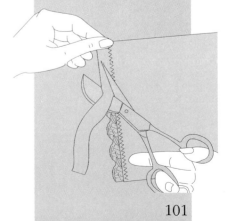

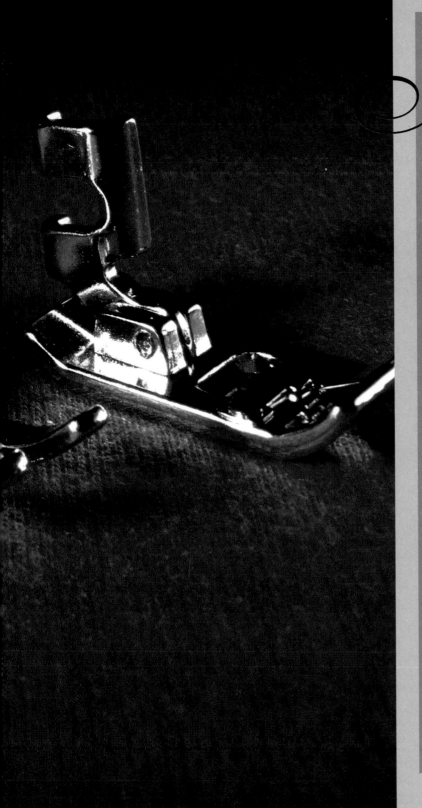

Needle
KNOW-HOW & FEET SMARTS

Having "needle know-how" and "feet smarts" can save you time and frustration while noticeably improving the quality of your sewing. In this chapter, I'll show you several needle and foot options and how to choose just the right combination for the task at hand.

Most home sewers use the standard all-purpose foot and a straight or zigzag stitch for 95% of their projects. Yet the accessory box that comes with your sewing machine contains a vast array of foot possibilities. Start experimenting today—you'll discover new sewing shortcuts and expand your creative horizons!

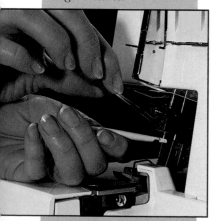

Needle KNOW HOW: WHICH ONE AND WHAT SIZE?

Universal-Point Needles

Use all-purpose needles for general sewing on both knit and woven fabrics. Universal needles are available in both American and European sizing. (American sizing is listed in parentheses.) Keep in mind that larger size numbers mean larger needle diameters.

Special-Purpose Needles

Stretch, Yellow Band, or ballpoint needles: Use these needles for tightly constructed knits, such as nylon/Lycra swimwear and cotton/Lycra blends. The special rounded point slides between the knit fibers, helping to prevent skipped stitches. Stretch needles are commonly available in sizes 75 (11) and 90 (14). For easy identification, these needles are often blue or have a blue or yellow shank.

Denim needles: As the name implies, these needles are engineered for sewing through dense fabrics like denim. Because the point of the needle is extra sharp, it can pierce the compact, heavy threads of the fabric. Common sizes are 90 (14) and 100 (16).

Leather needles: These special-purpose needles have a knife-edge cutting point so that they can easily sew through leather. But if used on fabric, they will cut holes. So don't use leather needles on synthetic suedes or other fabrics. A common size is 90 (14).

Topstitching needles: These needles, which are available in size 90 (14), have an

Needle Size European (American)	Fabric Weight	Fabric Types
60 (7)	Delicate	Silk, silk-like fabrics, voile
70 (9)	Lightweight	Lightweight polyester, microfibers
80 (12)	Medium-weight	Cotton, cotton blends
90 (14)	Medium- to heavyweight	Corduroy, wool
100 (16)	Heavyweight	Denim
110 (18)	Super-heavyweight	Upholstery fabrics

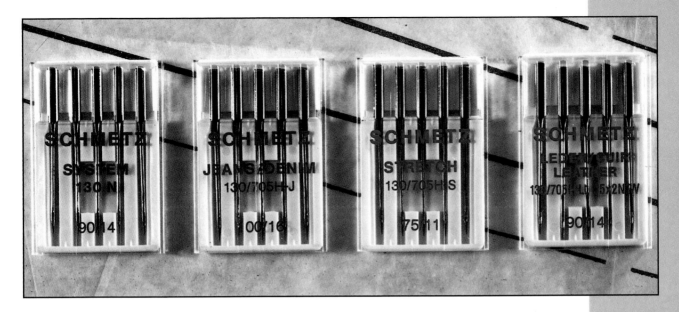

extra-large eye. The large eye allows button-hole-twist thread or 2 strands of all-purpose thread easy passage without fraying.

Double or Twin Needles

Probably the most popular of all specialty needles, double needles produce perfectly parallel rows of stitching, every time. Double needles will fit any zigzag machine that threads from front to back. Because the needles are fixed a certain distance apart, the lines of stitching are sewn simultaneously and the distance between the 2 rows never changes. Double-needle topstitching is a great way to add a tailored accent to casual clothes and edges of knit garments.

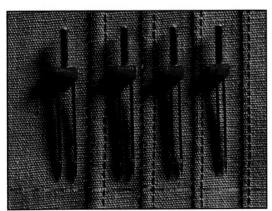

Double needles are available in sizes from 1.6 mm to 4.0 mm. The numbers indicate the amount of space between the needles. Sometimes double needle sizes are listed with 2 numbers, such as 4.0/100. In this case, the first number refers to the distance in millimeters between the 2 needles, while the second number represents the size of each needle.

Below are some common double needle sizes and their uses.

Sizes	Uses/Fabrics
1.6 mm	Pin tucking—delicate fabrics
2.0 mm	Pin tucking—delicate fabrics
3.0 mm	Pin tucking/topstitching—light- to medium-weight fabrics
4.0 mm	Topstitching—medium- to heavy-weight fabrics
6.0 mm	Topstitching—Use only on machines with 6.0 mm-wide throat plate openings.
2.5 mm-Stretch	Topstitching/hemming—light- to medium-weight knits
4.0 mm-Stretch	Topstitching/hemming—medium- to heavyweight knits

To thread your machine:
• Use 1 spool of thread on each of the spool pins on top of the machine.
• If your sewing machine has only 1 spool pin, wind extra bobbins and stack the bobbins on the spool pin.
• Following the threading instructions for your machine, guide both threads as 1 through the tension disk and thread guides. At the needle, separate the threads and insert 1 thread through the eye of each needle.

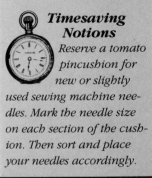

Timesaving Notions

Reserve a tomato pincushion for new or slightly used sewing machine needles. Mark the needle size on each section of the cushion. Then sort and place your needles accordingly.

Feet SMARTS

Zigzag Foot

Most of us are familiar with the zigzag foot, because it is the multipurpose foot most commonly used for everyday sewing. This foot has a wide opening, proportionate to the width of the zigzag stitch. The opening can range from 4 mm to 6 mm in width, depending on the machine.

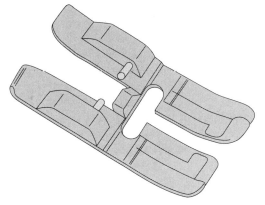

The throat plate used with the zigzag foot has an opening of similar size so that the needle can easily enter the bobbin area and form a perfect stitch.

accurately and to machine-quilt. It's easy to see where you're stitching when you are stitching "in-the-ditch" with the straightstitch/jean foot.

Straightstitch/Jean Foot

The straightstitch/jean foot has a single, small round opening in the center of the foot, just large enough to accommodate the needle. A throat plate with a corresponding small, round opening should be used in tandem with the foot.

This foot is useful when stitching slippery fabrics, to prevent your fabric from being forced down into the feed dogs. The tiny opening also minimizes puckering and creates a more uniformly balanced stitch.

The straightstitch/jean foot is also helpful to quilters. It can be used to join quilt pieces

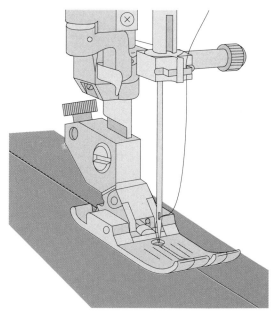

Note from Nancy

Since different brands of machine feet differ in appearance, don't worry if the ones provided with your sewing machine don't look exactly like the feet illustrated in this chapter. Rather, consider the common characteristics described for each and look for a foot in your accessory box with these characteristics.

Note from Nancy

When using the straightstitch/jean foot and throat plate, always make sure that the machine is set for a straightstitch. Any other stitch setting will cause the needle to hit the presser foot and break!

Straightstitch Foot Alternative

Don't despair if a straightstitch foot and throat plate aren't included in your sewing-machine accessory box. It's possible to gain the benefits of a straightstitch foot while using the multipurpose zigzag foot. I find this alternative especially important when topstitching through layers of heavy fabric. Here's how:

1. Attach the zigzag foot and adjust the machine for straightstitching.

2. Move the machine needle position from the center to the left position.

To ensure an accurate seam width, measure the distance from the needle to the seam line edge of the fabric. (Because the needle is offset to the left, the markings on the throat plate, which are set for a center needle position, will be incorrect. Unless an adjustment is made, the seam will be wider than desired.) Adjust the placement of the seam line as necessary.

3. Stitch the seam.

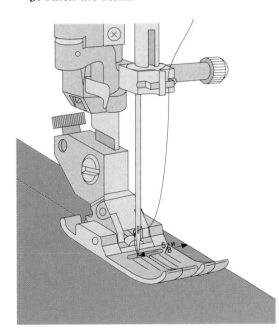

Blindhem Foot

The blindhem foot has an adjustable guide that will accommodate a variety of fabric weights and textures. The guide can be moved closer to or farther from the left side of the foot.

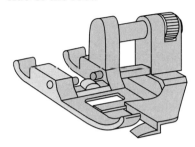

The blindhem foot is among the most versatile feet in your accessory box. In addition to the traditional use of hemming woven and knit fabrics, this foot can be used for applying patch pockets and producing super-straight edgestitching.

Blindhemming Woven Fabrics

When it is set for a blindhem, the machine will make several straight stitches, followed by 1 zigzag stitch. This pattern will be repeated for the length of the seam.

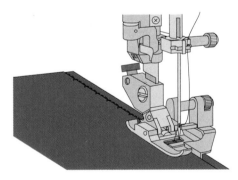

1. Thread the machine, using monofilament thread on top and thread matched to the color of your fabric in the bobbin.

2. To stitch the blindhem:

• Mark the hemline. Trim the hem allowance to the desired width; press the hem to the wrong side of the garment.

• Adjust the machine for blindhemming. (See your owner's manual for your specific settings.)

• With the wrong side of the garment facing up, fold back the hem allowance so that ⅜" to ½" of the hem's edge is visible to the right of the foot.

Note from Nancy

A stitch is formed when the needle thread enters the bobbin area and interlocks with the bobbin thread, which is located at the left side of the bobbin case. The closer the needle comes to the bobbin hook, the greater the likelihood of obtaining perfectly uniform stitches. Moving the needle to the left position places it as close as possible to the bobbin hook.

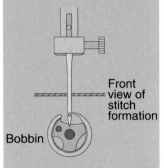

Front view of stitch formation

Bobbin

Note from Nancy

Many sewing machines offer a second blindhemming stitch for hemming knit fabrics. This stitch is composed of several narrow zigzag stitches followed by 1 wider zigzag. This adds the crosswise stretch needed for knit fabrics and helps prevent popped blindhem stitches.

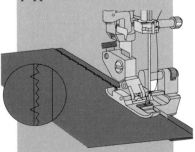

Timesaving Notions
Monofilament thread, available in clear and a smoke tint, blends readily with most fabrics and is nearly invisible on the right side of the completed hem. However, monofilament thread is made of nylon and is very heat sensitive. The hem must be covered with a press cloth before pressing.

• Guide the blindhem foot next to the fold. As you straightstitch into the edge of the hem, the zigzag should barely catch a thread in the fold of the garment fabric. Make a test sample to ensure that the stitching is inconspicuous on the right side. On the sample, move the adjustable guide on the foot to the right to take a deeper bite or to the left to take a shallower bite of the garment fabric. Remember, the deeper the bite, the more the zigzag thread will show on the right side.

"Handpicked" Patch Pockets—A Blindhemmed Shortcut

A blindhem stitch can be used to replace topstitching or edgestitching when you are applying a patch pocket.

To produce the "handpicked" stitch:

1. Use monofilament thread or thread matched to the color of your fabric in the needle, and use matching thread in the bobbin.

2. Adjust the blindhem stitch for a narrow width. The zigzag stitch should barely catch a few threads of the pocket, and the straightstitches should be hidden along the edge of the pocket.

3. Stitch along the pocket edge.

Another Blindhem Foot Trick— Even Stitching, Every Time!

Achieve perfectly straight topstitching or edgestitching, using the blindhem foot as a guide.

1. Adjust the blindhem guide so that the needle will stitch along the edge of the fabric.

2. Set the machine for a straightstitch. Guide the edge of the fabric along the blindhem foot guide; stitch.

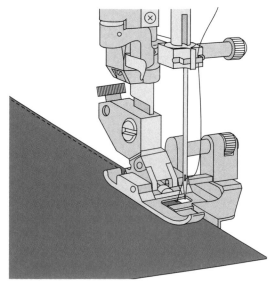

Quick, Blindhemmed Button Loops

Combine elastic thread and a blindhem foot to make button loops for little girls' dresses, bridal gowns, and evening wear.

1. Attach the blindhem foot. Adjust the machine for a blindhem stitch. Adjust the stitch length according to the size of the buttons to be used on the garment—use a shorter stitch for small buttons and a longer stitch for large buttons. (You may need to experiment on a scrap of fabric to find the right stitch length.)

2. Place the finished edge of the garment (parallel to the button area) and the elastic thread next to the guide of the blindhem foot. (You'll be sewing from the bottom to the top edge of the button placket.)

3. Stitch along the finished edge of the garment. The straightstitches will catch the garment. The zigzags will stitch off the fabric fold, catching the elastic thread and forming the button loops.

4. Securely handstitch the elastic at the top and bottom of the seam.

5. On the other side of the garment, sew small buttons that will fit through the elastic loops.

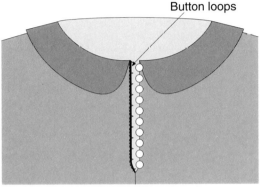

Button loops

Timesaving Notions

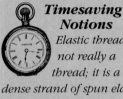

Elastic thread is not really a thread; it is a dense strand of spun elastic. Because of its thickness, it can't be threaded through the eye of the machine's needle. Innovative uses for elastic thread include zigzagging or serging over the elastic to stabilize a shoulder or to create smocking.

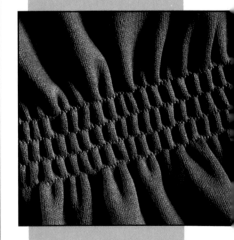

Embroidery Foot

The embroidery foot has an open toe. The toe may be completely open or its center may be clear plastic. This makes it easy to see the stitches as they are formed on the fabric.

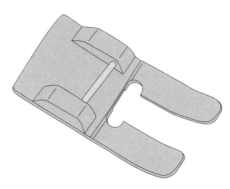

The underside of an embroidery foot has a hollowed or grooved section that allows the dense embroidery stitching to move smoothly under the foot without bunching up under the needle. Traditionally, the embroidery foot has been used for appliqué and decorative stitchery, but it also has many other creative applications.

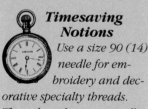
Timesaving Notions
Use a size 90 (14) needle for embroidery and decorative specialty threads. These threads are generally finer than all-purpose sewing thread, yet they still fray easily in a machine needle with a small eye.

Decorative Stitches

Customize your fashions or home furnishings by adding decorative machine stitching. Take advantage of all those stitch designs available on your machine and create some unique, personalized items.

• Loosen (decrease) the machine tension by 2 numbers or notches. This ensures that the top thread will float on the fabric surface, while the tighter bobbin thread is pulled invisibly to the underside.

• Insert a new machine needle and attach the embroidery foot.

• When you are working with a single layer of fabric, stabilize it with a piece of

Stitch-N-Tear or Wash-Away underneath. Or press the waxed side of freezer paper to the wrong side of the fabric with a warm iron; it will temporarily adhere to the fabric.

• Use rayon or cotton embroidery threads. Or, for a more lustrous appearance, try metallic embroidery thread.

• Remove the stabilizer after stitching.

Stitchery Magic—Change Colors Without Changing Thread

Although decorative stitches embellish fabric beautifully, we usually must change the thread to change the color. Here's an ingenious way to add color to specific areas without changing threads—use variegated thread!

1. Attach the embroidery foot and adjust the machine for the chosen decorative stitch.

2. Thread the machine with variegated thread; advance the thread through the needle to the desired color.

3. Stitch the portion of the design intended for that color.

4. When that portion is completed, stop with the needle in the down position.

5. Raise the presser foot to allow the

thread to move easily through the machine guides. Advance the thread between the tension disk and the needle to the color needed for the next portion of the design.

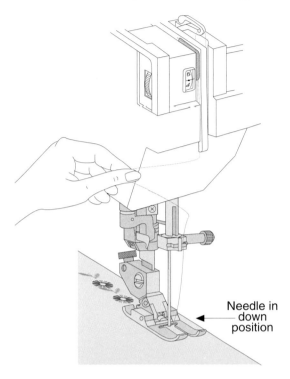

Needle in down position

6. Lower the presser foot. Raise the needle and advance the thread through the needle.

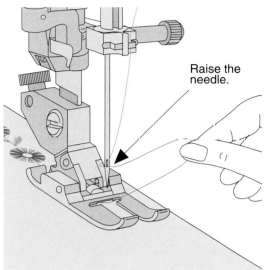

Raise the needle.

• Stitch the next portion of the design.
• Repeat until the entire embroidered section is completed.
7. With a hand-sewing needle, draw the loose threads to the underside. Knot the thread tails and clip off the excess.

Note from Nancy

Always test your stitching to be sure that the design is exactly the way you want it. After choosing your thread and decorative stitch, try them on a scrap of the project fabric before working on the actual project.

Pin Tuck Foot

The most distinctive feature of a pin tuck foot is the series of grooves on the underside. Depending on the manufacturer, the foot may have 5 to 9 grooves. These grooves provide channels or guides for previous rows of pin tucking. By combining a pin tuck foot with a double needle, it's simple to make row after row of straight, uniform, pin tucks.

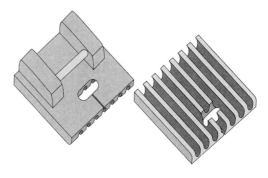

Lightweight fabrics like batiste are best for pin tucked garments such as children's clothing or heirloom sewing projects. (Use a size 1.6 mm or 2.0 mm double needle on these lightweight fabrics.)

Quick Corded Pin Tucks

To make the pin tucks more defined, add cording. Pearl cotton, topstitching thread, and crochet cotton are examples of cording that work well to make tucks more defined. Keep in mind that if the color of the cording contrasts with that of the fabric, it creates an intriguing shadowed effect.

1. Replace the standard needle with a double needle.

2. From underneath, insert the cording through the small circular opening on the throat plate, in front of the feed dogs. Use a serger looper threader or dental floss threader to draw the cording through the opening. Allow the rest of the cording to remain on the spool or cone so that it can easily feed through the machine. (Place the cording spool or cone on the table or floor in front of the machine.)

3. With a washable marking pen, mark the first row of pin tucks on the right side of the fabric. Because this first row will be the guide for all successive rows, it's extremely important that this first row be straight.

Monograms—The Easy, Decorative Way

Create attractive, professional-looking monograms in minutes by using your machine's decorative stitches. Try this technique on towels, pillow cases, and garments. (Remember, always test monogram stitching on a scrap of fabric before using it on the project.)

1. Transfer the initial(s) to the fabric with a washable marker.

2. Back the fabric with a stabilizer such as Stitch-N-Tear or Wash-Away.

3. Select the desired decorative stitch. Consult the instructions for your machine and drop the feed dogs if necessary. Stitch along the outline of the monogram.

• Gently and evenly guide the fabric for the smoothest curves and angles.

• Combine various stitches in the same monogram, if needed or desired.

4. When the monogram is completed, clip the loose threads. Tear away the stabilizer and remove any visible markings.

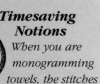

Timesaving Notions

When you are monogramming towels, the stitches may get buried in the nap of the towel. To prevent this problem and to achieve more even stitching, use a layer of Wash-Away stabilizer on both the top and the bottom of the towel. For extra ease in following the monogram, outline the initials on the top layer of the stabilizer instead of on the towel. After you finish stitching, just remove both layers of stabilizer.

Timesaving Notions

As the name implies, a Serger Looper & Needle Threader is used mainly to thread the loopers and needles of a serger. But the long, curved shape makes it a perfect notion to fit through the opening in the throat plate and draw the cording through the tiny hole. So you may want to keep more than 1 threader on hand!

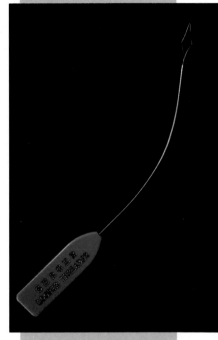

4. Stitch along the marked line.

• Begin stitching at least ¼" from the edge; this prevents the stitches and fabric from being drawn down into the bobbin area. As you stitch, the cording is secured to the wrong side of the fabric, inside the tuck, between the fabric and the zigzagged bobbin thread.

• Stitch slowly, because the bobbin thread must zigzag back and forth between the 2 needle threads.

5. For succeeding rows of stitching, align the first pin tuck in 1 of the grooves on the pin tuck foot. (The position depends on the desired distance between rows of stitching.) Stitch. Since the first pin tuck row follows the groove, subsequent rows will be straight and parallel to the first row.

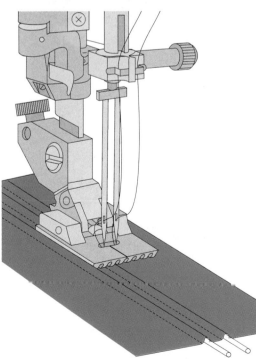

Tailor Tack Foot

The appearance of this foot varies slightly from machine to machine. It is characterized by a vertical raised bar that runs down the center of the foot. The machine stitches over this bar, creating loops.

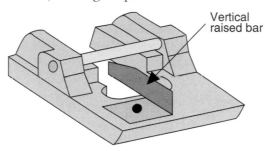

Vertical raised bar

But this versatile foot makes more than tailor tacks. It's a real time-saver when you are sewing on buttons and attaching shoulder pads, too.

1. Adjust the machine for button sewing, if possible. If no such setting is available, adjust the machine for a zigzag stitch and lower the feed dogs.

2. Tape the button to the garment.

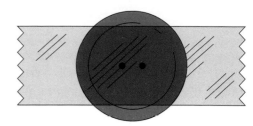

3. Place the garment under the presser foot, centering the tailor tack foot over the holes in the button. Lower the foot and turn the wheel by hand several times to test the width of the zigzag stitch. Adjust the stitch width if necessary.

4. Stitch through the holes of the button several times. If the button has 4 holes, reposition the foot and stitch through the remaining 2 holes.

5. When the stitching is completed, remove the garment from the machine, leaving extra long thread tails.

6. Remove the tape. Pull the thread tails through the button holes, to the space between the garment and the button. To make the thread shank, wrap the tails around the threads under the button. Tie the thread tails in a knot and clip the ends. Seal with Fray Check.

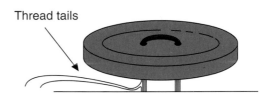

Thread tails

Fast, Efficient, Machine-Sewn Buttons

When you use the tailor tack foot to sew on buttons, you must use the sew-through kind of buttons with holes from front to back—and they must be flat with no shanks. But you can easily create thread shanks for the buttons. Button shanks make it possible for a blouse's buttonhole placket to fit under the buttons without puckering.

Shortcut: Secure Shoulder Pads with Machine Stitching

Using the same settings as those used for sewing buttons, you can attach shoulder pads to the seams of any garment. Just think of it—no more handstitching! The thread shank created by the tailor tack foot allows the pad to move, eliminating the dimples that can form on the outside of the garment if the pads are sewn in too tightly.

1. Pin the shoulder pads into position.

2. Use the tailor tack foot to stitch the corners of the pad to the sleeve seam allowances and the center of the pad to the shoulder seam allowance.

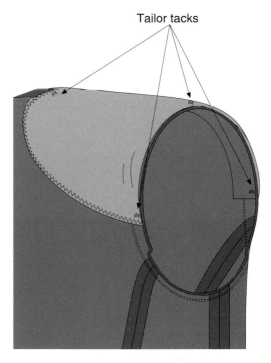

Tailor tacks

Overcast-Guide Foot

If you don't own a serger and you find that zigzagged edges curl and pucker, try using an overcast-guide foot. A special metal bar in the center of the foot's zigzag opening holds the fabric flat while the zigzag goes over the edge of the fabric. This foot also has a vertical bar that serves as a guide for fabric edges. Simply set the machine for a zigzag, guide the edge of the fabric along the guide bar, and stitch.

Discover this foot's potential for finishing the edges of napkins, tablecloths, and

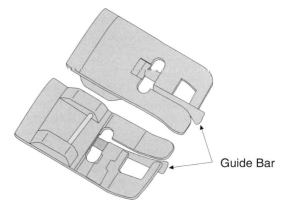

Guide Bar

scarves. Sewing takes slightly more time than serging, but you can closely simulate the appearance of a serged edge.

1. Set the machine for a satin stitch, using a wide stitch width and a short stitch length.

2. Satin-stitch each edge individually. Do not pivot at the corner; stitch off the edge.

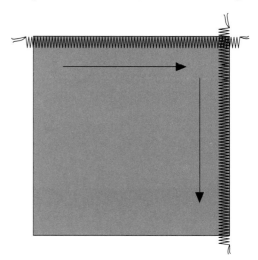

3. Use a drop of Fray Check at the corners to prevent the satin stitching from raveling. Allow the sealant to dry and clip the thread tails.

Felling Foot

This foot is characterized by an opening or groove through which fabric can easily be guided and turned under as it passes through the machine.

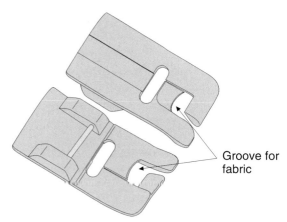

Groove for fabric

As you might imagine, the felling foot was originally designed for making flat-felled seams. With this foot you can easily duplicate these professionally tailored seams. In addition, you can apply ribbon to fabric for special accents.

Note from Nancy

Turn the machine's wheel by hand a few times to ensure that the zigzag clears the metal bar on the overcast-guide foot. If the stitch isn't wide enough, the needle may hit the bar and break.

Note from Nancy

The key to making this seam is to press under half of the width of the seam allowance so that it can be more readily guided into the felling foot. With some fabrics, finger-pressing at the beginning of the seam is all that's necessary; on others, it's advisable to press the entire seam with an iron. Test to see which works best.

Note from Nancy

Depending on the position of the groove on the felling foot, it may be necessary to change the position of the needle so that the ribbon is centered between the double needles.

Making a Flat-Felled Seam

All raw edges of a flat-felled seam, such as those seen on jeans or casual wear, are enclosed. The seam allowance on 1 side is wrapped over and encases the raw edge of the other seam allowance.

1. Stitch a ⅝" seam with *wrong* sides of the fabric together. Press the seam to 1 side (generally toward the back of the garment).

2. Trim 1 of the seam allowances to ¼".

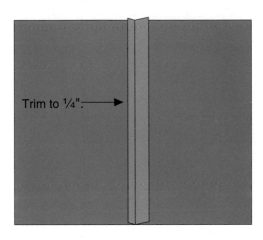

Trim to ¼".

3. Fold the remaining seam allowance in half and tuck the raw edge under the trimmed seam allowance, so that it encases the cut edge. Press.

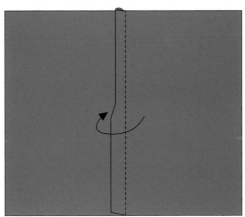

4. Stitch, guiding the fold of the seam along the groove of the felling foot.

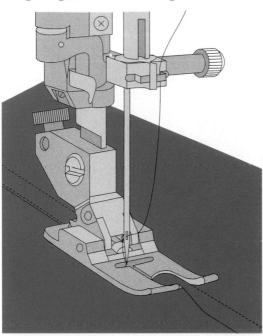

Instant Ribbon Accents

The felling foot, ribbon, and a double needle are all you need for this technique.

1. Insert a wide double needle (3.0 mm to 4.0 mm) and use 2 spools of thread through the top tension guides and needle eyes.

2. Insert a length of ¼"-wide ribbon into and through the slot in the felling foot.

3. Stitch the ribbon to the garment, guiding it along the groove as the 2 needles stitch it in place.

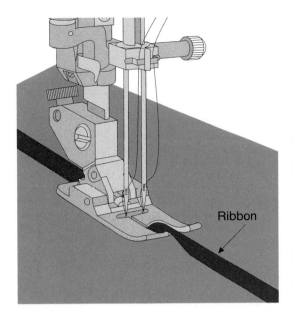

Ribbon

4. If a felling foot is not available for your machine, use the embroidery foot to achieve the same results. Guide the ribbon through the groove on the underside of the foot.

Single Cording Foot

The single cording foot is usually an optional accessory that can be purchased from your sewing machine dealer. The front of the foot, with a wide opening for the zigzag stitch, looks much like the standard zigzag foot. But to distinguish this foot, turn it over: The underside of the cording foot has a large, hollowed-out groove to accommodate cording, piping, or decorative trim, allowing it to lie flat and feed evenly under the foot.

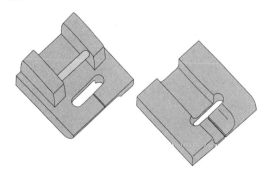

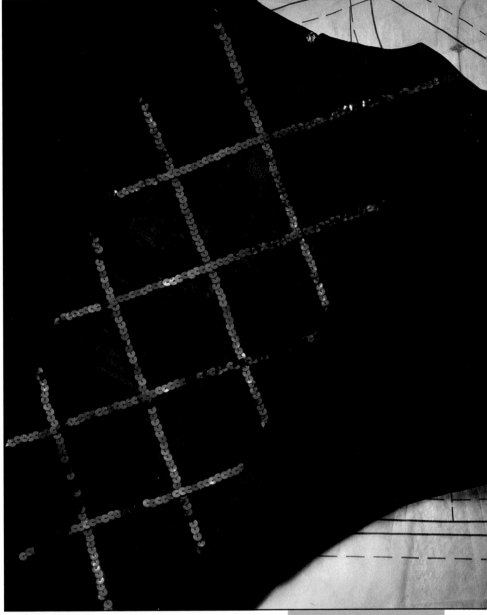

A Machine Shortcut: Apply Sequins or Beads by the Yard

Lend a festive look to garments, home-decorating projects, and craft projects by trimming with sequins or beads. Simply use your machine and the cording foot to easily stitch them in place!

1. Mark the placement of the sequins or beads on the right side of the garment. (To eliminate puckering, use Wash-Away or Stitch-N-Tear stabilizer on the back of lightweight fabrics.)

2. Position the sequin or bead strip along the placement lines.

• Since sequin strips have a nap, it's important to place the smooth direction running with the direction of the seam. Run

117

your finger along the sequin strip; if your finger catches the edges of the sequins, reverse the direction of the strip so that the sequins don't "fight" the groove of the cording foot. Always give a "test pat" before you start!

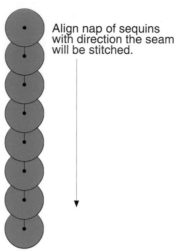

Align nap of sequins with direction the seam will be stitched.

• When you are applying beads, minimize bulk by removing the beads within the seam allowances.

3. To set up the machine:

• Attach the cording foot.

• Adjust the length and width of the zigzag so that the stitch is wide and long enough to clear the sequins or beads.

• Loosen the upper tension, especially when you are applying trim to lightweight fabrics.

• Thread the top tension guides and the needle with monofilament thread, metallic thread, or sewing thread in a color to match the fabric.

4. Place the sequins or beads in the groove of the foot. Stitch.

5. To apply several parallel rows of sequins or beads, use a quilting bar. Following directions in your owner's manual, attach the bar to the sewing machine's presser bar. For perfectly straight and evenly spaced

rows, guide the edge of the bar along the previous row of beading or sequins.

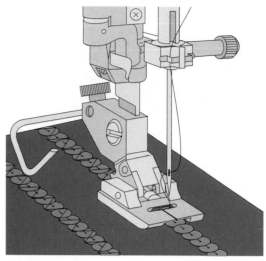

Perfect Machine-Sewn Piping

Here's an easy way to create and insert piping on fashions, furnishings, and craft projects.

1. To make the piping:

• Cut bias strips 2" to 2½" wide by the needed length. Cut cording the same length as the bias strips.

• Align the lengthwise edges of the strip, wrong sides together, and sandwich the cording inside the fold of the bias strip.

• Attach the cording foot. Position the cording so that it fits in the groove on the foot.

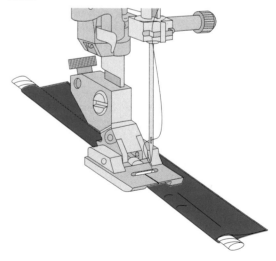

• Adjust the position of the sewing machine needle so that the stitching is close to the edge of the cording. Stitch.

• Mark ⅝" from the stitching line. Trim along this line so that the width of the piping seam allowance corresponds to the width of the garment seam allowance.

2. To insert the piping into the seam:

• Sandwich the piping seam allowance between the 2 garment seam allowances, with right sides and cut edges of the garment together.

• Place the cording in the groove on the underside of the cording foot.

• Change the needle position so that it lies close to the piping and aligns with the initial row of stitching. Measure to ensure

that the needle will stitch ⅝" from the raw edge of the fabric.

• Stitch through all layers. The seam is stitched and the piping is simultaneously inserted.

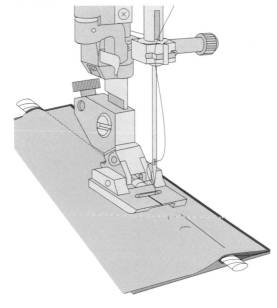

Note from Nancy

Usually piping is applied in a 2-step process; the piping is sewn to 1 side first and then the seam is sewn together. When you use this specialty foot, the groove saves a step and makes it a 1-step rather than 2-step process.

Begin
TO SEW

For those of you who are just beginning to sew or would like to teach others to sew, I've outlined here the basic "start-up" information. With the help of these guidelines, the satisfaction of your first sewing or teaching success is only a few steps away!

DETERMINING YOUR *Pattern* SIZE

Take Your Measurements Accurately

To select the correct pattern size, take these key body measurements.

To ensure accurate measurements:

• Ask someone to help you. It's almost impossible to hold the tape accurately by yourself.

• Measure to the closest ½".

• When taking width measurements, place a thumb or finger underneath the tape measure to prevent the measurement from being taken too tightly.

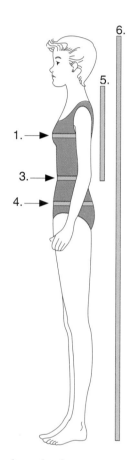

To take these body measurements:

1. Bust line—Measure around the fullest part of the bust line, keeping the tape measure parallel to the floor.

2. High bust line—Measure under the arms, across the back, and across the top of the bust line.

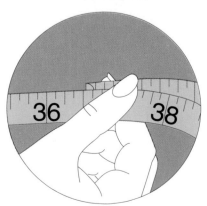

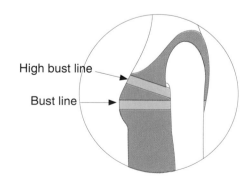

High bust line

Bust line

3. Waistline—Bend to the side; the deepest wrinkle is your waistline. Stand straight again and measure around your waistline, keeping the tape measure parallel to the floor.

4. Hipline—Measure the fullest part of the hipline, keeping the tape measure parallel to the floor.

5. Back waist length—Measure from the base of your neck to the waistline. Find the base of your neck by bending your head forward until the prominent bone at the base of the neck is easily felt. Straighten your neck and measure from that bone down your back to the waistline.

6. Height—Stand barefoot with your back to a wall. Lay a ruler flat on top of your head. Mark where it touches the wall. Then measure from the mark to the floor.

Buy the Right Size

Your figure and the type of pattern that will fit you best are determined by your body proportions. The standard body measurement charts are featured in the back of each company's pattern catalog. Compare the height, the back waist length measurement, and the description of the pattern type to your own proportions.

Key Sizing Measurements

For tops, dresses, jackets, and jumpsuits, use your bust line measurement as the sizing key. Compare your bust measurement to the size listed under your figure type.

Patterns are sized for a B bra cup. If your bust measurement is more than 2½" larger than your high bust measurement, it means you are larger than a B cup size. If this is the case, use the high bust measurement as your bust measurement when you purchase your pattern. The neckline and shoulder areas will fit better, although you may have to enlarge the bust line.

For pants, skirts, and culottes, consider the measurement that is critical to the fit of the garment when choosing the pattern size. For example, choose a pattern by the hipline size if the fit is tailored through the hipline. Or choose by the waistline measurement if the waist is fitted and the hipline is gathered or pleated.

Misses'

Misses' patterns are designed for a well-proportioned and developed figure, about 5'5" to 5'6" without shoes.

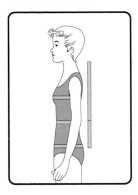

Petite-able

These patterns are appropriate for the shorter Misses' figures, about 5'2" to 5'3" without shoes. Bust, waist, and hip measurements are the same as those for Misses' patterns.

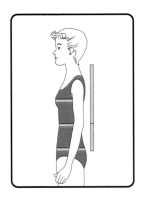

Half-size

Half-size patterns are for a fully developed figure with a short back waist length, about 5'2" to 5'3" without shoes.

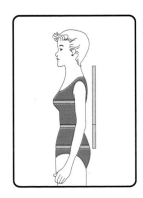

Note from Nancy

For toddlers, children, teens, boys, and men, refer to the corresponding size charts in the back of most pattern catalogs.

Note from Nancy

If your measurements fall between sizes, buy the smaller size if you are small-boned and the larger size if you are large-boned. Keep in mind that it is always easier to make the pattern larger through the bust line, waistline, and hipline than it is to make it smaller in the neckline and shoulder. My rule is: When in doubt, buy the smaller size!

Women's

Women's patterns are designed for the larger, more fully mature figure, about 5'5" to 5'6" without shoes.

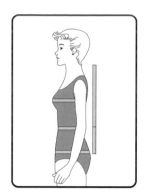

Young Jr./Teen

This size range is designed for developing pre-teen and teen girls' figures, about 5'1" to 5'3" without shoes.

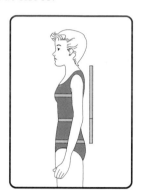

Pattern Size Charts

MISSES'

	XS		S		M		L	
Size:	6	8	10	12	14	16	18	20
Bust:	30½	31½	32½	34	36	38	40	42
Waist:	23	24	25	26½	28	30	32	34
Hip:	32½	33½	34½	36	38	40	42	44
Back Waist Length:	15½	15¾	16	16¼	16½	16¾	17	17¼

PETITE-ABLE

Size:	6	8	10	12	14	16
Bust:	30½	31½	32½	34	36	38
Waist:	23	24	25	26½	28	30
Hip:	32½	33½	34½	36	38	40
Back Waist Length:	14½	14¾	15	15¼	15½	15¾

HALF-SIZE

Size:	10½	12½	14½	16½	18½	20½	22½	24½
Bust:	33	35	37	39	41	43	45	47
Waist:	27	29	31	33	35	37½	40	42½
Hip:	35	37	39	41	43	45½	48	50½
Back Waist Length:	15	15¼	15½	15¾	15⅞	16	16⅛	16¼

WOMEN'S

Size:	38	40	42	44	46	48	50
Bust:	42	44	46	48	50	52	54
Waist:	35	37	39	41½	44	46½	49
Hip:	44	46	48	50	52	54	56
Back Waist Length:	17¼	17⅜	17½	17⅝	17¾	17⅞	18

YOUNG JR./TEEN

Size:	5/6	7/8	9/10	11/12	13/14	15/16
Bust:	28	29	30½	32	33½	35
Hip:	31	32	33½	35	36½	38
Back Waist Length:	13½	14	14½	15	15⅜	15¾

Tips SHOPPING

Pattern Selection—
Keep It Simple

Pattern catalogs and magazines offer an enticing selection of ready-to-sew fashions. Because your pattern will be the "road map" for your project, the catalog area should be your first stop at the fabric store.

For your first venture into sewing, select a simple garment. The conveniently tabbed sections of the catalog direct you to specific categories of fashion and size. Look for a category marked "easy-to-sew" or "learn-to-sew"; you'll find shorts, pants, skirts, jumpers, and tops especially designed for beginning sewers.

Valuable
Information on the
Pattern Envelope

After choosing a pattern style, study both the front and the back of the envelope. The front of the pattern envelope shows photos or sketches of all of the variations of the style included in the pattern. These photos or sketches, called "views," usually show the garments from the front.

Turn the envelope over and you'll discover a wealth of information.

Note from Nancy

Selection of fabric can be an overwhelming experience for novices (and even for experienced sewers), especially with the array of beautiful fabrics displayed at most stores. Don't hesitate to ask a sales clerk if you need assistance in finding the types of fabrics recommended for your pattern.

125

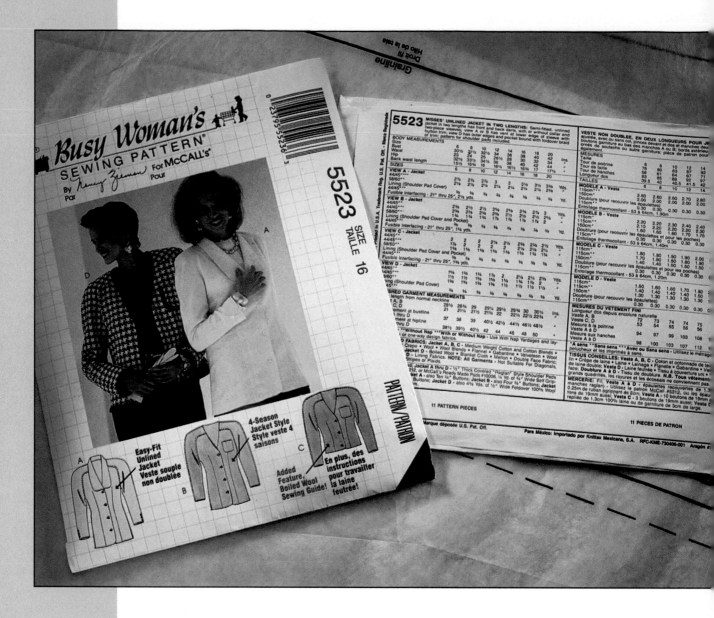

Back views: The styling of all the back views may be illustrated on the back of the envelope. Details such as darts, pockets, and variations in length are easily distinguished at a glance.

Body measurements: The envelope will have a concise chart of body measurements, usually including measurements for bust line, waistline, and hipline along with the corresponding pattern size.

Suggested fabrics: This is usually only a few lines, but it contains essential information—the designer's fabric recommendations. The suggested fabric recommendation also guides you away from certain fabrics that are less likely to work for this pattern style.

Phrases like "for stretch knits only" and "not suitable for diagonals" provide important information for you to use in your fabric selection.

Yardage chart: To determine the amount of fabric and interfacing to buy, you'll have to know 3 things: the pattern view (generally designated by a letter), your size, and the fabric width. Under the desired view, follow the size chart down and the fabric width chart across. The columns intersect at the yardage requirement.

Notions: The notions required to make your garment—buttons, snaps, hooks and eyes, zippers, elastic, and thread—will be listed in the "notions" section.

Before
YOU CUT OR SEW

Valuable Information Inside the Pattern Envelope

You'll find the pattern guide sheet and the tissue pattern pieces inside the pattern envelope. Think of the guide sheet as your instruction book for constructing this garment. The guide sheet includes:

• Illustrations of all the pattern pieces for the different pattern views.

• An explanation of symbols and terms used in marking the pattern pieces.

• A fabric key to identify the right side, wrong side, interfacing, and lining. These shadings vary from pattern company to pattern company.

• General information about interfacing, adjusting the pattern, cutting and marking, and sewing.

• Cutting layouts or illustrations that show how to place the pattern pieces on the fabric before you cut them out.

• Step-by-step instructions and illustrations showing how to make the project from start to finish.

Tissue Pattern Basics

Now unfold the pattern pieces and take out the pieces needed for the view you've selected. (If 2 or more pieces are printed on

Note from Nancy

Because it's easy to confuse all the different pattern layouts, circle the layout on the guide sheet for your size in the design view you've chosen. It's a simple step that can save frustration later.

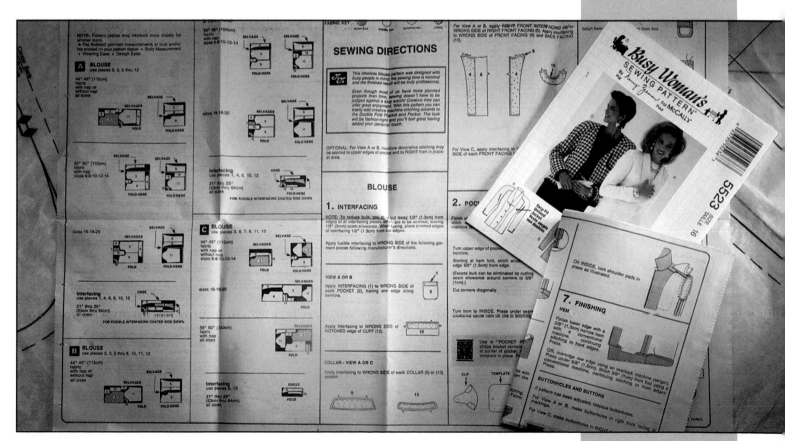

the same sheet, simply cut out the pieces you need, leaving a margin of tissue around each piece. You don't need to cut exactly, since you will trim the excess tissue to the cutting line when you cut out the garment.) Return the other pieces to the envelope.

Press the pattern pieces with a warm, dry iron to remove any wrinkles that might distort the shape of the pattern pieces when you cut out the garment. Separate the larger pattern pieces from the smaller ones.

Familiarize yourself with the symbols printed on the pattern. Think of them as highway signs—thcy hclp you get where you want to go.

• **Cutting line**—a solid, dark outer line. A pair of scissors is often drawn at intervals on the cutting line.

• **Stitching line**—a broken line drawn $5/8"$, $3/8"$, or $1/4"$ inside the cutting line. This is the line on which you will sew.

• **Grain line arrow**—an arrow printed on the pattern piece to help you correctly align the pattern on the fabric. The arrow must lie parallel to the grain (usually lengthwise) of the fabric.

• **Fold line**—a thinner line than the cutting line, drawn parallel to the edge of the pattern piece. It usually has at each end a double-ended arrow that points to the actual fold line. "Place on fold" is generally printed along the arrow.

• **Notches**—single or double diamonds with corresponding numbers. Notches help you match garment pieces accurately when you sew.

• **Circles and squares**—additional marks that also help you align and match garment pieces more precisely. These marks may indicate points at which to start or stop stitching.

• **Other lines**—Special lines, such as hemline, center front, center back, and fold lines, show placement of construction details. "Lengthen or shorten here" lines show recommended positions for adding length to or subtracting it from the pattern without changing the lines or fit of the garment.

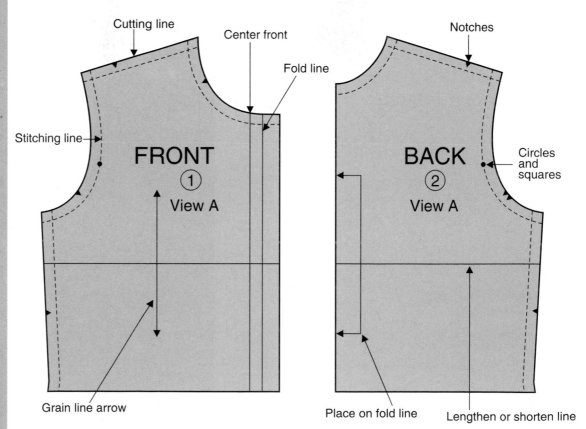

Layout & Cutting Tips

The guide sheet shows how to place the pattern pieces on the fabric. There will usually be several pattern layouts to choose from. Select the correct layout according to the view you've chosen, your size, and the width of your fabric.

Follow the instructions in the guide sheet and lay out the larger pattern pieces along the grain line of the fabric. At 1 end of the printed grain line arrow, measure the distance from the arrow to the fabric fold. Make sure both ends of the arrow measure the same distance from the selvage. Pin the pattern to the fabric at each end of the arrow to keep it from moving as you lay out the remaining pieces.

If a pattern piece has a "Place on fold" line, place the line exactly on the fold of the fabric. Pin the pattern to the fabric along the fold line, with the pins at right angles to the fold. Extend the heads of the pins over the edge of the fold; this will prevent you from cutting into the fold by mistake.

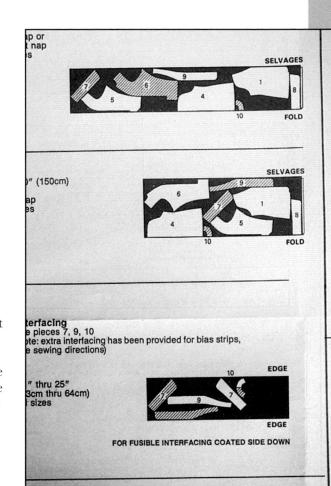

SELVAGES

FOLD

SELVAGES

FOLD

terfacing
e pieces 7, 9, 10
te: extra interfacing has been provided for bias strips,
e sewing directions)

" thru 25"
3cm thru 64cm)
sizes

EDGE

EDGE

FOR FUSIBLE INTERFACING COATED SIDE DOWN

Lining (Shoulder Pad Cover and Pocke
use pieces 3, 11

44" 45" (115cm)
fabric
without nap
all sizes

Interfacing
use pieces 2, 9, 10
(note: extra interfacing has been prov
see sewing directions)

21" thru 25"
(53cm thru 64cm)
all sizes

C **JACKET**
use pieces 1, 2, 4, 5, 6, 9, 10

44" 45" (115cm)
fabric
with nap
all sizes

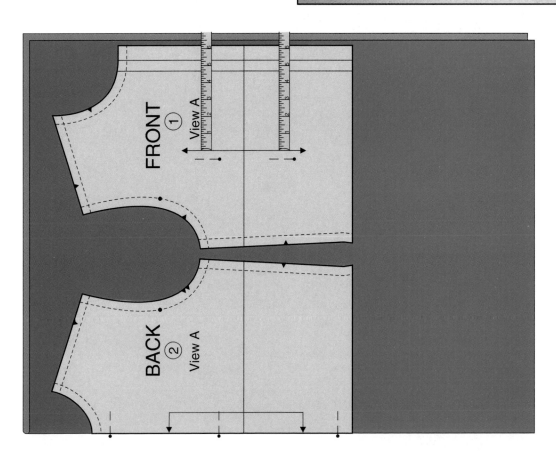

To pin the smaller pattern pieces to the fabric:

1. Position the pattern piece on the fabric. Then place a pin diagonally in each corner.

2. Pin from corner to corner, placing the pins parallel to the cutting line (but not on the line), every 6" to 8".

3. Use extra pins around curved areas and on smaller pieces.

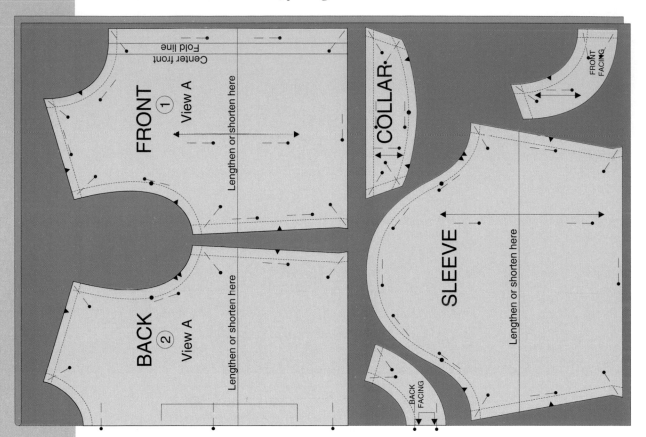

SUCCESSFUL SEWING Basics

I recommend that you refer to the pattern guide sheet for step-by-step sewing instructions. Place the guide sheet in a location that is easy to see and reach.

Try pinning it to a bulletin board mounted on the wall behind your sewing machine. Then use a thumbtack to mark which step you are sewing. After you finish that step, move the tack to the next step. When you return from a break, the tack will make it easier for you to pick up where you stopped.

Remember, the guide sheet is just that—a guide. Feel free to try different techniques, to vary the order of construction, and to construct the garment in time units (as discussed in Chapter 1).

Seams—Elementary, But All-Important

Seams are the most basic construction element. Chances are, if you seam successfully, you will sew successfully. Here's how:

1. Align the seam notches and the cut edges of the garment pieces, with right sides together.

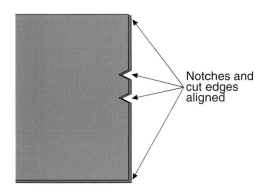

Notches and cut edges aligned

2. Pin the 2 layers of fabric together, with the pins perpendicular to the edge of the fabric. Place pins with the point in and the head toward the pattern edge.

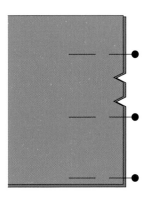

3. Begin and end each seam by locking the stitches. Sew 2 or 3 stitches with the stitch length set at 0 (or the shortest length available).

4. Change the stitch length to 10 to 12 stitches per inch (the normal setting) for the rest of the seam.

5. When you are machine-stitching long seams along the lengthwise grain of the fabric, sew from the bottom of the garment to the top. (For example, on the side seams of a skirt, stitch from the hem to the waistline.) Sewing from the widest to the narrowest part of the garment is frequently referred to as "directional stitching" in sewing publications. Directional stitching is recommended because the machine is sewing with the grain of the fabric; stitching against the grain could cause the fabric to stretch or pucker.

6. Remove pins as you come to them. Do not sew over them; you might damage or break your machine needle.

Seam Finishing Options

Fabric that ravels needs a seam finish to prevent fraying, especially if the finished garment will be machine-laundered. Here are some recommended ways to finish seams.

• **Zigzag** over the cut edges. Stitch with a medium-width zigzag and a medium-to-short stitch length. Stitch the "zig" in the fabric and the "zag" off the cut edge. Hold the raw edge taut while zigzagging to help prevent tunneling (the "scrunching" that occurs when the fabric is drawn up by the side-to-side zigzag action).

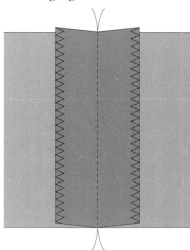

• **Serge** the edges with a 3- or 3/4-thread overlock stitch. This is the newest, fastest and neatest seam finish available to home sewers. (Refer to Chapter 3 for more information on serging.)

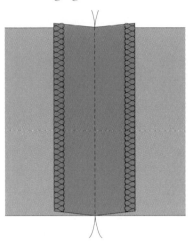

• **Trim** the edges with pinking shears. Pinking is perfect for lightweight, tightly constructed fabrics (such as silk and silk-like fabrics), but this seam finish will not effectively discourage raveling on loosely woven fabrics.

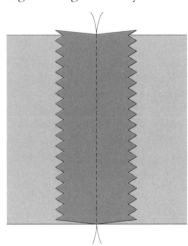

Fast, Professional Pressing

Pressing techniques are just as important as sewing techniques. Keep this general guideline in mind: Never join 2 seams together without pressing both seams flat first, just as they were sewn, and then pressing them open. This smooths the stitches and embeds them into the seam.

Prevent the edges of lengthwise seams from making an imprint on the right side of a garment by pressing the seam over a sleeve roll.

Timesaving Notions

A sleeve roll is a long, sausage-shaped pressing tool with a cotton cover on 1 side and wool on the other. If you do not have your own sleeve roll, tightly roll a magazine into a tube and cover it with fabric.

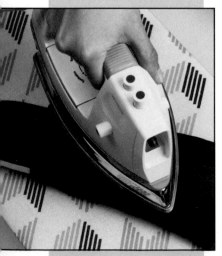

Smooth and Durable Darts

Darts, which are used for shaping the garment fabric to body contours, are triangular folds, with wide ends tapering to a point.

To sew a smooth and durable dart:

1. Mark the point of the dart with a pin. Fold the dart with right sides together, matching the nip markings at the cut edge.

2. Place the cut edge of the fabric under the presser foot and lower the needle. (Always stitch darts from the cut edge toward the point.) Do not lower the presser foot yet.

3. Pull the top thread to form an 8" to 12" thread tail. Lower the presser foot and lay the thread on top of the fabric to mark the stitching line between the clips and the dart point.

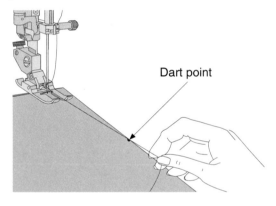

Dart point

4. Lock the threads to begin the dart. Lengthen the stitch to normal length and, following the thread guide, finish stitching the dart.

5. At the end of the dart, turn the machine's wheel by hand, barely catching 3 to 4 stitches along the fold.

6. Tie the thread by sewing off the fabric, allowing the threads to lock together (called "chaining").

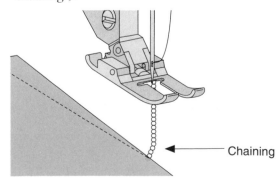

Chaining

After chaining 1" to 2", sew the chained thread tail to the dart. Sew 2 to 3 stitches in the dart to secure the threads. Then trim the thread ends.

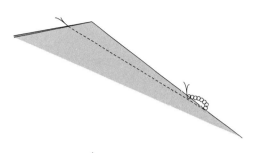

My Favorite Gathering Method

The pattern guide sheet generally recommends stitching 2 basting rows and pulling the threads (either top or bobbin) to gather fabric. While this is definitely a workable technique, the gathering threads have an annoying tendency to break.

Instead, try this method—a favorite of mine—when your pattern guide sheet calls for gathers:

1. Place the fabric under the presser foot. Turn the wheel by hand to take 1 complete stitch in the fabric. Bring the bobbin thread to the top side by lightly pulling on the top thread. The bobbin thread will appear as a loop coming through the fabric.

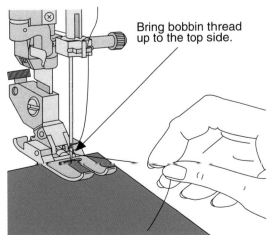

Bring bobbin thread up to the top side.

2. Pull the bobbin and top threads to measure as long as the area to be gathered. Gently twist the 2 threads together.

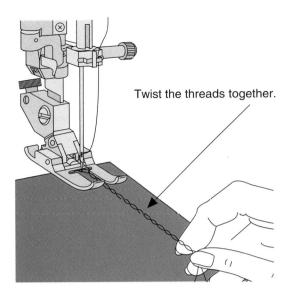

Twist the threads together.

3. Adjust your machine for a wide zigzag and short stitch length. Zigzag over the twisted threads inside the seam allowance, making a "casing" for the gathering threads. Make sure you don't stitch through the twisted threads.

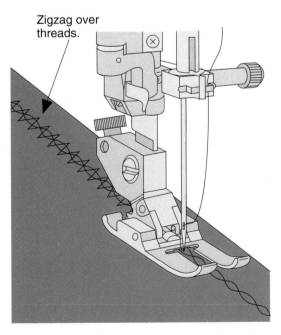

Zigzag over threads.

4. Gather by pulling the twisted threads. Because the threads are anchored in the first stitch, the gathering threads will not pull out of the fabric.

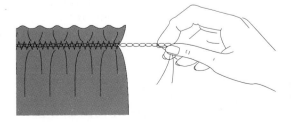

Note from Nancy

Here's another tip on stitching a straight dart:
- *Use a piece of lightweight cardboard, such as the cardboard that bias tape is wound on.*
- *Before lowering the presser foot, align the cardboard with the needle and the point at the end of the dart.*
- *Stitch along the edge of the cardboard.*

Glossary

ANCHOR CLOTH: A multi-layer fabric scrap sewn over before sewing on heavy fashion fabric. Using the anchor cloth prevents the beginning of a line of stitching from bunching up or jamming. After the seam is completed, the cloth is clipped away.

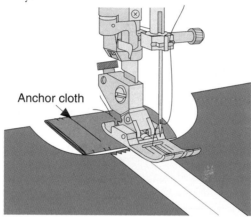

Anchor cloth

APPLIQUÉ PRESSING SHEET: A reusable nonstick sheet used with an iron when bonding fusible webbing to the wrong side of fabric.

APPLIQUÉ SCISSORS: Scissors that have a 6" duck-bill blade and are usually used for cutting appliqué work. To trim the excess fabric from an appliqué or a seam allowance, the duck-bill blade is placed under the fabric to be trimmed so that the wrong layer is not accidentally cut.

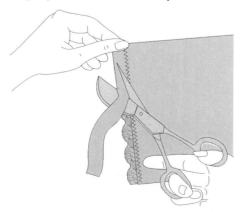

BACKSTITCH: To secure stitches at the beginning and end of each seam, which prevents them from coming out. Sew 2 or 3 stitches, adjust the machine to stitch in reverse, sew 2 or 3 stitches, and then proceed with the seam.

BAR-TACK: To stitch in place to secure facings or sew on buttons.

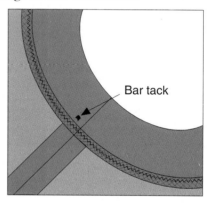

Bar tack

BASTING: Long running stitches used to hold 2 or more layers of fabric in position while seaming. The temporary stitches are removed after the final stitching is done.

BIAS: A diagonal line between the lengthwise and crosswise threads on a fabric. A true bias lies at a 45° angle to the selvage and has more stretch than lengthwise or crosswise grains.

BLADES: Parts of a serger that cut the fabric as it is stitched. One blade remains stationary while a second blade moves up and down in synchronization with the needle(s).

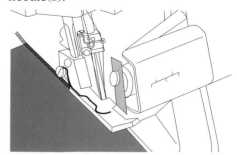

BLINDHEM STITCH: A machine stitch formed using a special blindhem foot and stitch setting. The machine makes several straight stitches followed by 1 zigzag stitch, repeated along the entire hem.

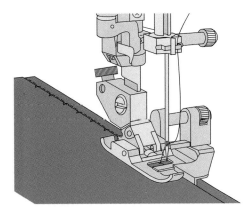

BOBBIN: A case that holds the lower thread in a conventional sewing machine.

BODKIN: A tool used to insert ribbon, lace, or elastic into a garment casing.

BRAIDED ELASTIC: The most economical of elastics. Because it narrows when stretched, it should only be used in casings.

CASING: A tube, formed by 2 layers of fabric connected by 2 or more rows of stitching, in which elastic or a drawstring is inserted.

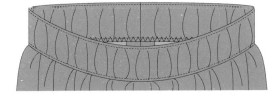

CHALK OR CHALK WHEEL: Tool used for marking darts, pleats, and button or buttonhole placement on the fabric.

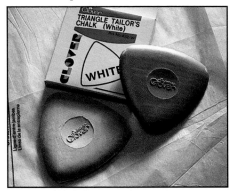

CLEAN-FINISH: To finish the cut edges of a seam by zigzagging, serging, pinking, or encasing the edge with a fabric tape.

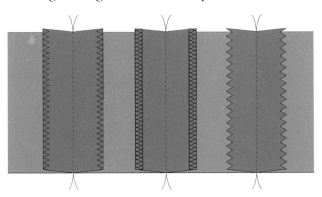

CLIPS: Short cuts made perpendicular to the seam line after joining 2 garment pieces. Clips are used to help curved pieces lie flat after being turned.

CONED SERGER THREAD: Two-ply thread used primarily in sergers. Because this thread is lighter in weight than all-purpose thread, it reduces bulk at the seam line.

DOUBLE NEEDLES: Two needles joined together at 1 shank, used for decorative stitching. The needle threads stitch in a straight line, while the bobbin thread zigzags between the 2 needle threads. Double needles are also known as twin needles.

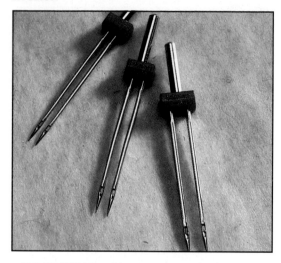

EDGESTITCH: To straightstitch close to the edge of a seam.

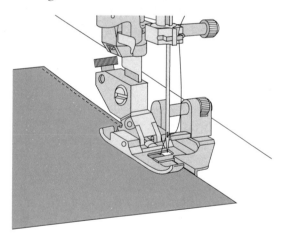

ERASER EASING: A method of easing fullness using 2 pencil erasers to grip and stretch the fabric.

FACING: A garment piece that covers and encloses a raw edge.

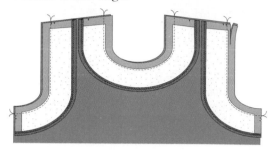

FEED DOGS: Teeth-like grippers nestled in the throat plate of a sewing machine or serger. The feed dogs move back and forth to feed the fabric through the machine as stitches are formed.

FINGER-PRESS: To apply pressure to a seam by compressing the fabric layers between your thumb and index finger.

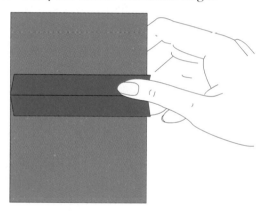

FLATLOCKING: A serging technique that uses 2 or 3 threads with very loose thread tension on the wrong side of the garment. Two layers of fabric are serged together and then gently pulled until the fabric is flat.

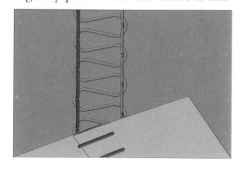

FUSIBLE INTERFACINGS: Interfacings treated with a special heat-activated resin. When pressed, a fusible interfacing is bonded permanently to the wrong side of the fashion fabric.

FUSIBLE WEB (FUSIBLE-TRANSFER WEB): Heat-sensitive adhesive fibers applied to a peel-away paper backing. The web is fused to 1 side of the piece to be applied, the paper backing is peeled away, and the fresh surface of the web is then fused to the garment or backing fabric. It saves time when applying fabric appliqués, positioning pockets, and fusing hemlines.

GATHERING: A wide zigzag stitched over the top and bobbin threads used to pull fabric into soft folds. Gathering is used to control large amounts of fullness when joining a large section of fabric to a smaller one.

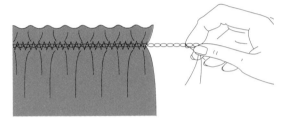

GRADING: Cutting each seam allowance a different width to reduce bulk. Facing seams are generally trimmed to ¼" and garment seams to ⅜".

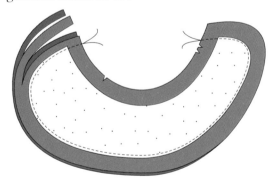

GRAIN: The lengthwise and crosswise threads of a woven fabric. The lengthwise grain is parallel to the selvage and has the least amount of stretch. The crosswise grain is perpendicular to the selvage and has a little more give.

GRAIN LINE: Indicated on a pattern by an arrow that aligns with the lengthwise or crosswise grain of the fabric.

GRIDDED CUTTING BOARD OR MAT: A mat made of a special "self-healing" material that is not damaged by the blade of a rotary cutter. The cutting board protects the work

surface and is a must when using a rotary cutter.

GRIDDED RULER: A heavyweight, transparent plastic ruler marked with horizontal and vertical lines for ease in measuring. The gridded ruler is used with a rotary cutter and cutting board.

HANDPICKED POCKET OR ZIPPER: In this shortcut, a machine blindhem stitch replaces topstitching or edgestitching when applying a patch pocket or zipper to a garment.

INTERFACING: A second layer of lightweight fabric added to the inside of a garment to give shape and body.

INTERLOCK: A lightweight, stretchable knit fabric constructed with 2 loops of yarn (1 loop knit from the back and 1 from the front of the fabric). Like other double knits, it looks the same on the right and wrong sides.

JERSEY KNIT: A single-knit fabric formed from 1 set of yarn loops. It is smooth on the right side, with horizontal loops running crosswise on the wrong side.

KNIT FABRICS: A lightweight fabric created by interlocking loops of yarn—1 loop of yarn pulled through another loop. Most knits stretch. Examples of knit fabrics include interlock, sweatshirt fleece, and sweater knits.

LOCK STITCH: Two or 3 stitches sewn in 1 place to secure threads.

LOOPERS: Devices found on sergers that handle the lower threads. Sergers have an upper and a lower looper, which interlock the threads in a knit-like fashion.

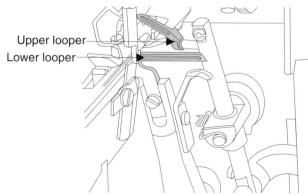

Upper looper
Lower looper

LOWER LOOPER THREAD: The last thread cone on the right on all except 5-thread sergers. The lower looper thread does not pass through the fabric. It passes underneath the fabric, catching the needle thread on the left and the upper looper thread on the right.

MITERED CORNERS: A method of finishing corners at a 45° angle to reduce bulk.

MONOFILAMENT THREAD: Lightweight nylon thread suitable for use in serging, sewing, or quilting when invisible stitching is required. Use the clear thread for light-colored fabrics, and the smoke tint for dark-colored fabrics.

MULTI-ZIGZAG: A variation of a machine zigzag stitch formed by 3 stitches in each direction. It is often used when a stretch stitch or understitching is recommended.

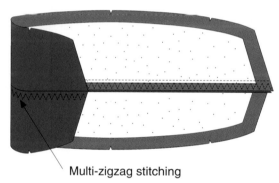

Multi-zigzag stitching

NIP: A ¼" clip cut into a seam allowance prior to sewing. A nip marks a notch, dart, tuck, fold line, or other important point on the fabric.

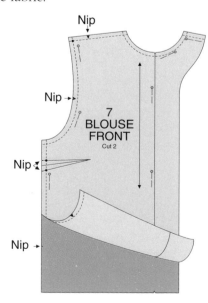

Nip

Nip

7
BLOUSE
FRONT
Cut 2

Nip

Nip

NON-ROLL ELASTIC: A type of knitted elastic that retains its shape and stays flat when stretched.

NONWOVEN FABRIC: A fabric formed from fibers forced together with heat, moisture, and pressure. Examples of nonwoven fabrics include polyester fleece, felt, and many interfacings.

NOTCH: A single- or double-diamond marking found on sewing patterns that is used to match garment pieces accurately. Notches are numbered in the order in which seams are to be joined.

ONE-WAY LAYOUT: A method of placing all pattern pieces for a garment in a single direction to avoid directional shading. One-way layouts are important when cutting napped fabrics (such as velvet or corduroy) and many jersey knits.

PATTERN WEIGHTS: Tools used as shortcuts in pattern cutting. Pattern weights eliminate the need to pin patterns to the fabric before cutting.

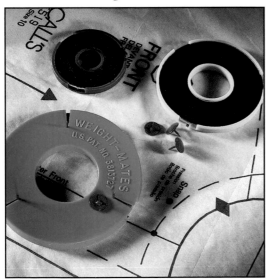

PINKING SHEARS: Shears with special serrated blades that cut a zigzag edge on fabric. Pinking reduces raveling on cut edges of fabric.

PIN TUCKS: A decorative effect consisting of rows of tiny, parallel fabric folds. Pin tucks can be sewn with a double needle on a conventional machine, or with a rolled-hem stitch on a serger. They are frequently found on heirloom-look blouses, children's wear, and decorator accessories.

PRESSER FOOT: The part of the sewing machine or serger that holds the fabric against the feed dogs as the stitches are formed.

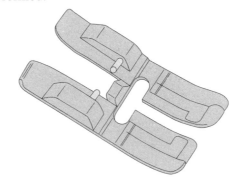

PRESSING SEAMS FLAT: The first step of the two-step procedure for pressing all seams—press the seam flat and then press it open. It will be easier to press the seam open if it first has been pressed flat.

PRETREATING: The process of washing and drying fabric prior to cutting and sewing. Pretreating reduces shrinkage in the final garment, removes resins from the fabric, and helps to prevent skipped stitches during sewing.

PUCKER: An undesirable bunching of fabric that usually occurs where 2 seams of different lengths are joined, such as the seam that joins the sleeve cap and the armhole.

QUARTER MARKS: Points indicated with pins or a washable marker to divide fabric into 4 equal parts. Quarter marks are used to position and distribute fabric evenly when sewing ribbing or elastic, for example, to the waist, neckline, or the sleeves of a garment.

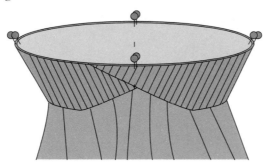

RAVEL-PROOFING ENDS: On serged seams, done by applying a drop of seam sealant to the beginning and end of the seam and then clipping the thread tail, or by using a darning needle to bury the thread tail under the looper threads.

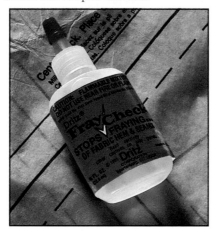

RIBBING: A knit fabric used to finish the neckline, waist, and wrists of T-shirts and sweatshirts.

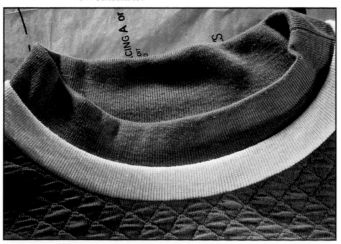

ROLLED EDGE: A decorative way to finish an edge using a 2-thread or 3-thread stitch on a serger machine. The rolled edge is created by an unbalanced tension, narrow stitch width, and short stitch length.

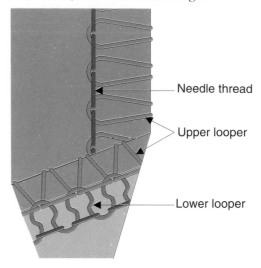

Needle thread

Upper looper

Lower looper

ROTARY CUTTER: A special fabric cutting tool which looks and works like a pizza cutter. Used in combination with a special cutting board and gridded ruler, it is used to cut several layers of fabric accurately.

SCISSORS: Cutting tools that have blades less than 6" long and have identical handle bows for the finger and thumb. Scissors are perfect for trimming, clipping, and crafts.

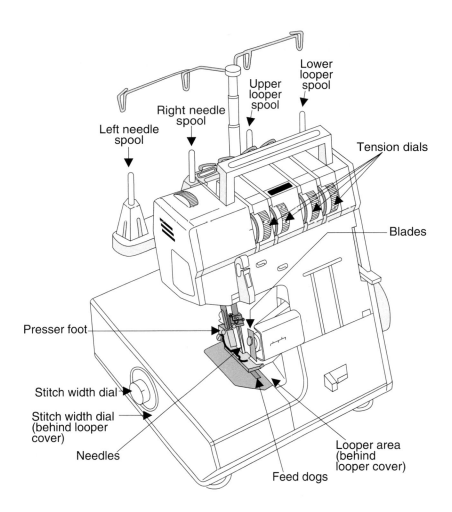

Left needle spool

Right needle spool

Upper looper spool

Lower looper spool

Tension dials

Blades

Presser foot

Stitch width dial

Stitch width dial (behind looper cover)

Needles

Feed dogs

Looper area (behind looper cover)

SEAM ALLOWANCE: The distance between the cutting line and seam line, usually ⅝".

SEAM LINE: Stitching line followed when sewing a garment. On pattern pieces, it appears as a broken line inside the solid cutting line.

SELVAGE: The tightly woven finished edges of fabric. Selvages do not ravel.

SERGED SEAMS: Seams finished on a serger with a 3- or 3/4-thread overlock stitch.

SERGER: A special sewing machine that uses 3, 4, or 5 threads instead of the 2 threads on a conventional sewing machine. It stitches a seam, finishes the raw edges, and cuts off excess fabric all at the same time.

SHANKS: Wrapped thread that connects a button to a garment. Button shanks make it possible for the button-hole placket to fit under buttons without puckering.

SHARPENING STONE: A tool used to sharpen shears and scissors periodically to ensure clean-cut edges.

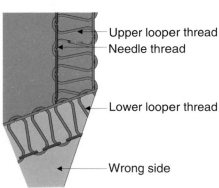

Upper looper thread

Needle thread

Lower looper thread

Wrong side

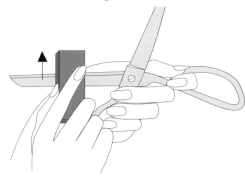

SHEARS: Cutting tools that have blades longer than 6" and have different-sized handle bows or loops (a small loop for the thumb and a larger loop for 2 or more fingers). Shears are perfect for cutting out fabric.

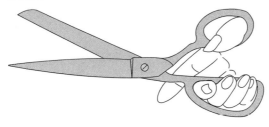

STABILIZER: A fabric strip used to give support and prevent undesirable stretch in stress areas such as the shoulder seam on knit garments. Common stabilizers are fusible interfacing and Stay-Tape.

STACKING: A technique of cutting out 2 different fabrics at the same time. For example, if you are making a lined skirt, stack the skirt and lining fabrics and cut out both at once.

STITCH IN-THE-DITCH: Stitching in the groove of a seam on the right side of the garment, through all thicknesses of the facing and garment. It prevents facings from rolling to the right side.

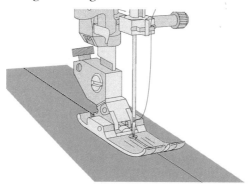

TEST SWATCH: A small square of fusible interfacing and fabric used to determine the suitability and fusing time required for your selected fabric and interfacing.

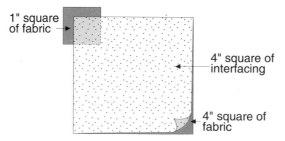

1" square of fabric

4" square of interfacing

4" square of fabric

THREADFUSE: A polyester thread twisted with a heat-activated fusible fiber. It bonds to fabric instantly with a touch of a steam iron.

TOPSTITCH: A decorative straightstitch on the right side of fabric, usually $\frac{3}{8}$" from the seam line.

TRIMMING: Cutting a seam within $\frac{1}{4}$" of a stitched seam to eliminate bulk. Trimming keeps a facing or an under collar from rolling to the right side.

UNDERSTITCH: Pressing seam allowances toward a facing or undercollar and then stitching on the facing, as close to the seam as possible, to prevent the facing from rolling to the right side.

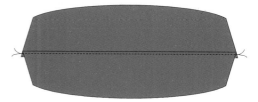

UNIVERSAL POINT NEEDLES: All-purpose sewing machine needles used for general sewing on knit and woven fabrics.

UPPER LOOPER THREAD: The second or third thread from the right on a serger. This thread does not pass through the fabric. Instead, it passes over the surface of the fabric, catching the needle thread on the left and the lower looper thread on the right.

V-CLIPS: Markings used to indicate center backs and fronts on garments, collars, and facings, as well as hemlines.

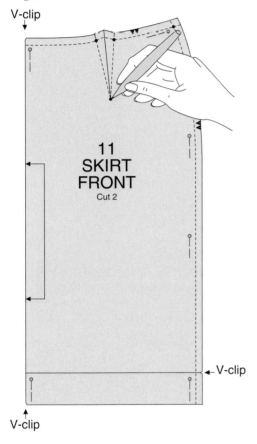

WATER- OR AIR-SOLUBLE MARKING PENS: Marking tools used to transfer pattern markings to fabric. The marks from water-soluble pens will disappear after being washed; the marks from air-soluble pens will disappear within 12 to 48 hours, depending upon the humidity in the air.

WATER-SOLUBLE STABILIZER: A temporary sheet of plastic fabric that dissolves in water. It is used to stabilize fabric and mark placement for embroidery or buttonhole stitching done by machine.

WOVEN FABRIC: Fabric made by interlacing threads over and under one another. Examples of woven fabrics include denim, corduroy, muslin, and broadcloth.

WRAPPED CORNER: A sewing technique used to eliminate bulk in corners. Two separate lines are stitched instead of 1 continuous line of stitching, with an angle at the corner. The seam allowances of the first stitching line are wrapped toward the facing or under collar and are then stitched over by the second line of stitching.

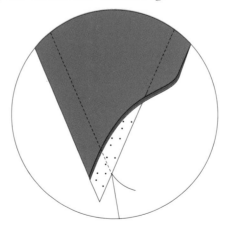

For a complete line of sewing notions turn to...

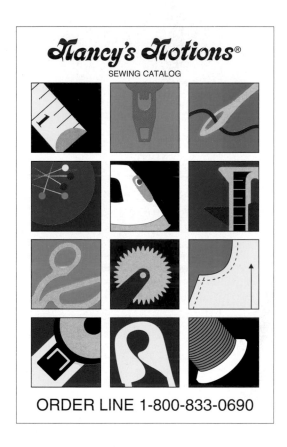